Ron Paul: Speaking of Freedom

Ron Paul: Speaking Of Freedom

J. Dorsett Miller

Published by Booksurge Publishing.

ISBN 1-4196-8538-4

Contents

The Old Man and the Internet

Ron Paul represents the beginning of a transition in American politics. Internet Candidacy has found its first real champion. Ron Paul has brought together the libertarian leaning centrists who have generally been a swing vote leaning Republican and Howard Dean's enthusiastic Internet oriented Democrats. These groups pride themselves on their rationality, and feel that there is something amiss in American public life. The unifying virtue is a philosophy which has been largely absent from American politics since the defeat of Barry Goldwater in 1964: Personal Responsibility.

A new rationality has formed within the active Internet community. Previous generations latched on to the ideologies of various parties in response to the threats and the continuously increasing complexity of the modern world. The active Internet community has largely grown up in that more complex world, and for the time being they feel that their capacity to understand is keeping ahead of the rate of change of society in general. They do not like questions of modern life to be unanswerable, they know where to get the answers they need, and are ready to share those answers with anyone who has the time to seek them.

The attacks of 9/11 created a temporary setback in this process of moving beyond the old ideologies. All Americans, the Internet community included, shifted to the right due to the fear and confusion the attacks created. But this shift to the right did not hold as long among active Internet users as it did among the general population, and now it has almost completely subsided. Perhaps George W. Bush could have held on to these people if he and his staff had been less secretive, more open to questions, and overall more competent. The Internet community does not just value openness, it expects it. When information is withheld from the community at large, suspicion grows rapidly and the circles of the Internet feed back on themselves generating speculation to fill the gap of knowledge. That speculation is almost always tinted with the suspicion engendered by the initial secrecy. This led George W. Bush to lose the confidence of the Internet community at large much faster than he lost the confidence of the American population as a whole.

Within the new rationality there are two large and easily distinguishable groups:

Internet Oriented Democrats

The Internet oriented democrats think of themselves as more rational than the traditional base of the democratic party. They feel that the traditional system of entitlements has failed, and that government has stagnated, held down by the inertia of its own bureaucracy. Their priorities are more in line with Bill Clinton and Jimmy Carter than with Ted Kennedy and

Nancy Pelosi. Party doctrine is uninteresting, and knee jerk fidelity to single issue interest groups is offensive. Compassion must be tempered with personal responsibility.

Libertarian Leaning Centrists

Similarly the libertarian leaning centrists think of themselves as more rational than the traditional base of the Republican party, especially the religious right. Indeed the reaction to the religious right has been negative and resentful for quite some time. The laissez-faire economic wing of the Republican party brought up the religious right, seemingly planning to manipulate them to their own ends. They did not comprehend the fact that once the religious right was mobilized it would bring the same zeal and will to power that it uses in its churches into the political arena. The centrist libertarian Internet users of today do not have memories of the Republican party of Goldwater. The Republican party they know seems opposed to individual rights, and pays lip service to personal responsibility. Religion is not irrelevant in these people's lives, it is simply no one's business except their own, and those politicians who create public policy in the name of religion seem to be either sickeningly calculated panderers or thoughtless zealots.

Ron Paul has become the champion of both of these groups. It has been said that Ron Paul's success is merely knee jerk support due to his opposition to the war. Others say it is merely an emotional response to his style in the Republican debates so far. Indeed both of these factors are part of the explanation for his success, but they are components in a much larger and more significant whole. The Internet community is developing its own political sensibility, a sensibility which goes beyond red and blue states and Red and Blue issues. This sensibility is grounded in a new rationality which has its genesis in the very structure of the Internet itself.

Internet Culture

Ron Paul has found success by targeting what, on face value, seems to be a niche market. Those people who orient themselves by the new rationality of the Internet see in Dr. Paul a kindred spirit. Ron Paul is at least four decades older than most of the Internet oriented individuals who make up his core supporters. He is a product of the Barry Goldwater school of thought. He ran for President under the libertarian ticket in 1988, when many of his current supporters were still in grade school. The fact that he can appeal to Internet users speaks volumes about the new rationality of the Internet. It does not matter his age, or the context in which he formed his ideas; all that matters are the ideas. Ron Paul did not rework his message to appeal to the Internet. His message is this: constitutional government, based on a document which is one of the most easily accessible in existence, the Constitution of the United States of America. He is willing to speak his mind without the obvious manipulative calculus that drives the mainstream candidates. He is the antithesis of George W. Bush in that he is opposed to secrecy and understands that honesty keeps the government healthy through accountability. The Internet community wants their questions answered, and they want them answered now. Ron Paul seems very willing to accommodate, and has been rewarded with support.

It is not surprising that the Classical Liberalism of strict constitutionalist government is so appealing today. The rise of the Internet has recreated many of the circumstances which allowed it to flourish in the eighteenth century. Classical liberalism developed as the old patriarchal structure of society began to break down. The absolute power of kings was no longer necessary for security. Similarly this new Internet oriented libertarianism is developing as the patriarchal structure of the Cold War world finishes breaking down completely. Creative and commercial success is no longer dependent upon the patronage of a huge corporation or government agency. Additionally, as with the eighteenth and early nineteenth centuries the development of the Internet has created a wealth of open space which can be acquired and worked by any

individual who desires to do so. Instead of open farm-
land, there is open intellectual space. The sense of
freedom of expression fostered by all this opportunity
has been the driving force behind the desire for
increased political freedom which has been manifest
since 2004. Ron Paul's movement has gained traction
by offering to fulfill this desire. Neither party has a
mainstream candidate who is as strong a proponent of
individual freedom as Ron Paul.

All of the major candidates feel inauthentic, most are
tainted by heavy corporate influence, and all are
caught up in the machinations of the government and
its bureaucracy. Most people are offended by bureaucracy and the power it has over us; Internet users are
especially offended. Bureaucracy is slow, secretive,
and mostly incompetent. The functionaries who
occupy government jobs are not held to standards of
personal responsibility, neither are the functionaries
who hold 90% of the jobs in large corporate bureaucracies. Internet users who have been forced to adapt
to these circumstances have become disheartened, but

unlike previous generations they have not surrendered their hopes to the will of the machine. The Internet oriented individuals have largely rejected the idea that having an unpleasant or meaningless job is inevitable. They change jobs often, and when they find one which is enjoyable they throw everything they have into it. Similarly these individuals are not satisfied with voting for the lesser of two evils in political races. They have rejected the mainstream candidates in the same manner they reject bad television shows, by simply ignoring them. Howard Dean woke them up in 2004. He got them to stop ignoring the situation entirely. Ron Paul is the natural successor, an authentic candidate with a new message that is, in fact, over 200 years old.

Internet oriented individuals have a mistrust of large organizations, especially of large organizations which are older than the Internet. Microsoft is rather broadly hated. The large telcos and the cable Internet providers are looked upon with suspicion. The mainstream press seems biased, sometimes to the left, sometimes to the right, but always to the sensational and meaningless. Authentic opinion and analysis comes from bloggers, not national commentators Hollywood is a vehicle for a few good movies and a lot of trash. The Internet appreciates the movies, and then rejects the trash that surrounds them for the most part. Most importantly for Ron Paul, the US Government is seen as an intruder in the eyes of most Internet users. The US Government has provided so much for the Internet, including the funding to get it started in the first place, but as the Internet moved into the mainstream, the government's policy towards the Internet has become restrictive, and is now seen as an instrument of the power of large, old corporations. Ron Paul offers a solution: Eliminate it all. This has a broad appeal, reaching deep into the heart of the Internet.

Personal Responsibility

You are responsible to your own reputation on the Internet. Your website is expected at the very least to be either entertaining, rational and convincing, informative, or novel. Preferably as many of these as you can achieve You are not expected to be clothed or to have showered while providing your novel entertainment that also informs and convinces. Your ideas are what matter, not your circumstances, your dress, or your car. Such things are inconsequential.

The founding fathers believed that men should be judged based on their willingness to work and their talents for thinking and producing. The aristocracy based on birth was replaced with one based on the agreement of the elite thinkers of the time. All men should have equal opportunities to succeed, and they should be judged on the success or failure of their actions. For the new community of elites, ideas are greater than actions. Consistent hard work must be coupled with creative interesting ideas or else it fails to inspire, and thus fails to garner support and investment.

Now, as then, money plays a great role in the new

order of things. In a process that began with the dot-com bubble, the old corporate aristocracy is being replaced by a new aristocracy of Internet elites. AT&T has been killed, chopped up, and resold; the big three automakers are stagnant or in decay; Microsoft is losing ground to Google as the essential software provider of the Internet world. The difference is the orientation towards the population in general. Old style corporations sought to homogenize American culture as they got larger and less capable of creative thought. The more homogeneous, the easier it is to sell a single product to the largest number of people.

The American car industry of the 1950's and 1960's had similarities to the culture of Internet companies today. There was upheaval as large companies consumed smaller ones, as the companies consolidated each brand held onto its own identity for a time. American cars were artwork, a new model each year with new features, added styling, each brand appealed to a distinct niche group of consumers. You could express your personal style with the car you drove.

Now, to an extent, you can express your personal style by the web portal you use. AOL is old and clunky, but does all kinds of things for you and works great for novices. Yahoo is the new AOL, doing all kinds of things for you without being as clunky or dumbed down. Google is the mainstream source for the Internet oriented individuals, with many niche spin offs of Google holding small die hard user bases.

The Internet provides an accessible outlet for creativity and expression with an audience whose size is determined by the quality of the material. When you're browsing, you do what you want. The soap opera on the television is far less interesting than the soap opera of your friends and acquaintances on Facebook or Myspace.

National television networks are finally taking notice of this phenomenon. By offering up many shows as podcasts they are gaining huge numbers of Internet viewers. Internet users are unwilling to be chained to the set schedule imposed by the television networks.

If an Internet user wants to sleep in on Sunday and watch Meet the Press at 2:00 AM, then all he needs is an Internet connection and iTunes.

File Sharing and Information Freedom

Everything is available free on the Internet if you're willing to work hard enough to find it. Internet users do not pay for content, they pay for the convenience of not having to go get it themselves. Internet services are SERVICES. There is no such thing as charging for a 'product' there is only charging for convenience and speed.

The New York Times web site recently eliminated its paid service, opening up all their columnists and most popular articles to the entire Internet community at large, just as they had been for years before the paid service was created. Their user numbers have reflected the change.

The cruelty of the Recording Industry Ass. of America

(RIAA) in dispensing random "justice" through its lawsuits has not stopped illegal file sharing. Its main result has been to infuriate the Internet community and all other decent minded people along with them. The RIAA is perhaps the best example of the old corporate world attacking the new system of Internet libertarianism. Certainly the record companies cannot be blamed for their angst at the prospect of losing their cherished system for distributing music to the world. It has been terribly profitable over the years as most enforced oligopolies are.

Individual music collections were previously composed of tangible products thus their distribution could be controlled. Those days are over and will never return. The idea that the record industry can replace individual CD sales with sales of Licenses through web sites is poor and will die out as the Internet continues to mature. Grasping at anything to keep them alive content providers have been seeking to control individual freedoms through licenses of increasingly senseless severity. From digitized book licenses that prohibit reading a book out loud to your child, to song licenses that prohibit humming a tune on the bus or subway, these corporations have abandoned innovation and creativity and have decided to sue Pandora's box until it closes again. Certainly we cannot blame the lawyers for promoting this strategy, as it is becoming terribly profitable for them, though not profitable for either the companies pursuing it or the artists who are obligated to them.

All new means of connecting people are used to try to connect their connectors. Right when humans started painting on walls, they started painting about sex. They don't show it on the discovery channel, but right there next to the guy throwing his spear at the buffalo is a painting of people getting it on. Writing, literature, drama, poetry, even the telephone, all were used to convey sexual ideas very quickly after their invention.

Google undoubtedly makes the most money each year off the Internet porn industry, and they don't have a single pornographic image stored on their servers. All they provide is the connections, and the market is willing to pay to have Google connect you to them. Speed and convenience is what the Internet is about, its what Google is about, and its what porn on the Internet is about.

Classical Liberal values flourish on the Internet because these are the primary concerns. Ron Paul appeals because he offers the hope that the government might abide by the same principals as the Internet community at large. As long as we aren't harming anyone, leave us alone. What you do in your home is your business, we don't care and we don't want to hear about it. John Ashcroft gets cold sweats at night imagining that somewhere, people are masturbating. That doesn't mean he should have been appointed attorney general in order to try to stop them. As long as they aren't hurting anyone else, the government shouldn't care at all. Regulation and litigation aren't the answer, the market polices itself.

Individualism Among the States

In the midst of a Ron Paul presidency, much power would devolve back to the states. The individual character of each state population would be reemphasized and a period of nation de-homogenization would likely occur. This would be refreshing, and likely do as much as anything in the Ron Paul government towards making America into a more vibrant and intellectually competitive nation. South Carolina might impose the death penalty for abortion, and ban all birth control pills. New Hampshire might eliminate all government welfare programs and shut down its public school system. California might institute a progressive agenda backed by its massive economy. Oregon and Vermont might legalize recreational marijuana and draw in a strange collection of citizens.

The parties in America have colluded with corporate interests for so long that the homogenization of America through consumerism has been integrated into the expectation that the federal government must rule on matters of moral decision. The expectation of being fed and clothed and entertained by corporate entities is not nearly so debilitating as the expectation that they will do our thinking for us.

Workers in America are increasingly information workers. Most of the best paying jobs in America can now be done from anywhere. A decentralization of decision making will allow these new liberated workers to locate themselves in communities that share their values. Company dress codes, working hours, long commutes and other vestiges of the old way of doing things exist now more out of habit than out of necessity for a large portion of the American workforce, especially those of middle incomes and higher. It doesn't matter if you develop web pages at from 8 AM to 5 PM, or from 2 AM to 10 AM, so long as the work gets done. Similarly, it doesn't matter if you live in a community centered around strict theological imperatives, or a community of hedonistic leisure and decadence.

Whether you live in your parents' house and work in your underwear, or live in a condo and work in a cubicle, your productivity and ability to contribute is all that should be judged. Thinking by numbers and measurable results will prevail in productivity situations.

This decentralization will also disarm a lot of the tensions in American society. By allowing people to segregate themselves along ideological lines by means of state governments the feelings of powerlessness and resentment harbored by those who hold strong ideological beliefs will be dispelled. When issues such as gay rights, abortion, welfare, and others can suddenly be decided at a local level the solution to the argument ceases to be vitriolic national campaigns which divide the nation and disillusion moderates. A gay man in a conservative religious state would be presented with 2 choices, fight the fight in the local government, or move. The important feature is that he can move, and that the prejudices of one state are not going to follow him to another of his choosing.

Federal government mandates are never going to decide issues like abortion and gay rights in a way that everyone is pleased. Thus they should not be federal issues. Federalist national government is not a good method for deciding the morals of groups of people. Local governments are closer to the community, more flexible, capable of more rapid change. Their bureaucracies, while still odious, are smaller, and less detached from the individuals they are charged with regulating.

Decentralization is the natural trend of the Internet age. The people who have grown up with the Internet know that individuals have the power to govern themselves. Our republic was designed with a very different set of considerations in mind, but now we have come to the point where old ideas are converging with the new. Decentralization of our governments will only accelerate.

Speeches of Dr. Paul

This section of the book is dedicated to the text of speeches which Dr. Paul gave before the House of Representatives and its committees. He is a great and thoughtful speaker. I have attempted a breif summary to highlight the various speeches; these can be found at the beginning of each section marked in the table of contents. I have also added commentary of my own upon them. Of his congressional speeches that I have read, I feel these are the best. They are reproduced here in their entirety.

A Republic, If You Can Keep It

**A speech by Ron Paul on Feb 1, 2000
on the floor of the US House of Representatives.**

1. Introduction

The dawn of a new century and millennium is upon us and prompts many to reflect on our past and prepare for the future. Our nation, divinely blessed, has much to be thankful for. The blessings of liberty resulting from the republic our forefathers designed have far surpassed the wildest dreams of all previous generations.

The form of government secured by the Declaration of Independence, the American Revolution, and the Constitution is unique in history and reflects the strongly held beliefs of the American Revolutionaries.

At the close of the Constitutional Convention in Philadelphia on September 18, 1787, a Mrs. Powel anxiously awaited the results, and as Benjamin Franklin emerged from the long task now finished, asked him directly: "Well Doctor, what have we got, a republic or a monarchy?" "A republic if you can keep it" responded Franklin.

The term republic had a significant meaning for both of them and all early Americans. It meant a lot more than just representative government and was a form of government in stark contrast to pure democracy where the majority dictated laws and rights. And getting rid of the English monarchy was what the Revolution was all about, so a monarchy was out of the question.

The American Republic required strict limitation of government power. Those powers permitted would be precisely defined and delegated by the people, with all public officials being bound by their oath of office to uphold the Constitution. The democratic process would be limited to the election of our leaders and not used for granting special privileges to any group or individual nor for defining rights.

Federalism, the binding together loosely of the several states, would serve to prevent the concentration of power in a central government and was a crucial element in the new Republic. The authors of the Constitution wrote strict limits on the national government and strove to protect the rights and powers of the states and the people.

Dividing and keeping separate the legislative, executive, and the judiciary branches, provided the checks and balances thought needed to preserve the Republic the Constitution created and the best way to preserve individual liberty.

The American Revolutionaries clearly chose liberty over security, for their economic security and their very lives were threatened by undertaking the job of forming a new and limited government. Most would have been a lot richer and safer by sticking with the King. Economic needs or desires were not the driving force behind the early American patriotic effort.

The Revolution and subsequent Constitution settled the question as to which authority should rule man's action: the individual or the state. The authors of the Constitution clearly understood that man has free will to make personal choices and be responsible for the consequences of his own actions. Man, they knew, was not to be simply a cog in a wheel, or a single cell of an organism, or a branch of a tree, but an individual with a free will and responsibility for his eternal soul as well as his life on earth. If God could permit spiritual freedom, government certainly ought to permit the political freedom that allows one to pursue life's dreams and assume one's responsibilities. If man can achieve spiritual redemption through grace, which allows him to use the released spiritual energy to pursue man's highest and noblest goals, so should man's mind, body, and property be freed from the burdens of unchecked government authority. The Founders were confident that this would release the creative human energy required to produce the goods and services that would improve the living standards of all mankind.

Minimizing government authority over the people was critical to this endeavor. Just as the individual was key to salvation, individual effort was the key to worldly endeavors. Little doubt existed that material abundance and sustenance came from work and effort, family, friends, church, and voluntary community action, as long as government did not obstruct.

No doubts were cast as to where rights came from. They came from the Creator, and if government could not grant rights to individuals, it surely should not be able to take them away. If government could provide rights or privileges, it was reasoned, it could only occur at the expense of someone else or with the loss of personal liberty in general. Our constitutional Republic, according to our Founders, should above all else protect the rights of the minority against the abuses of an authoritarian majority. They feared democracy as much as monarchy and demanded a weak executive, a restrained court, and a handicapped legislature.

It was clearly recognized that equal justice and protection of the minority was not egalitarianism. Socialism and welfarism were never considered.

The colonists wanted to be free of the King's oppressive high taxes and burdensome regulations. It annoyed them to no end that even the trees on their own property could not be cut without the King's permission. The King kept the best trees for himself and his shipbuilding industry. This violation of property ownership prompted the colonists to use the pine tree on an early revolutionary flag to symbolize the freedom they sought.

The Constitution made it clear that the government was not to interfere with productive non-violent human energy. This is the key element that has permitted America's great achievements. It was a great plan; we should all be thankful for the bravery and wisdom of those who established this nation and secured the Constitution for us. We have been the political and economic envy of the world. We have truly been blessed. The Founders often spoke of "divine providence" and that God willed us this great nation. It has been a grand experiment, but it is important that the fundamental moral premises that underpin this nation are understood and maintained. We as Members of Congress have that responsibility.

This is a good year to address this subject. The beginning of the new century and millennium provides a wonderful opportunity for all of us to dedicate ourselves to studying and preserving these important principles of liberty.

2. Success of the Republic

One would have to conclude from history as well as current conditions that the American Republic has been extremely successful. It certainly has allowed the creation of great wealth with a large middle class and many very wealthy corporations and individuals. Although the poor are still among us, compared to other parts of the world, even the poor in this country have done quite well.

We still can freely move about, from town to town, state to state, and job to job. Free education is available to everyone, even for those who don't want it nor care about it. Both the capable and the incapable are offered a government education. We can attend the church of our choice, start a newspaper, use the Internet, and meet in private when we choose. Food is plentiful throughout the country and oftentimes even wasted. Medical technology has dramatically advanced and increased life expectancy for both men and women.

Government statistics are continuously reaffirming our great prosperity with evidence of high and rising wages, no inflation, and high consumer confidence and spending. The US government still enjoys good credit and a strong currency in relationship to most other currencies of the world. We have had no trouble financing our public or private debt. Housing markets are booming, and interest rates remain reasonable by modern-day standards. Unemployment is low. Recreational spending and time spent at leisure are at historic highs. Stock market profits are benefiting more families than ever in our history while income, payroll, and capital gains taxes have been a windfall to the politicians who lack no creative skills in figuring out how to keep the tax-and-spend policies in full gear. The American people accept the status quo and hold few grudges against our President.

The nature of a republic and the current status of our own are of little concern to the American people in general. Yet there is a small minority, ignored by political, academic, and media personnel, who do spend time thinking about the importance of what the proper role for government should be. The comparison of today's government to the one established by our Constitution is a subject of deep discussion for those who concern themselves with the future and look beyond the fall election. The benefits we enjoy are a result of the Constitution our Founding Fathers had the wisdom to write. However, understanding the principles that were used to establish our nation is crucial to its preservation and something we cannot neglect.

3. The Past Century

Unbelievable changes have occurred in the 20th Century. We went from the horse and buggy age to the space age. Computer technology and the Internet have dramatically changed the way we live. All kinds of information and opinions on any subject are now available by clicking a few buttons. Technology offers an opportunity for everyone who seeks the truth to find it, yet at the same time, it enhances the ability of government to monitor our every physical, communicative, and financial move. And let there be no doubt, for the true believers in big government, they see this technology as a great advantage for their cause.

We are currently witnessing an ongoing effort by our government to develop a national ID card, a medical data bank, a work data bank, "Know Your Customer" regulations on banking activities, a National Security Agency all-pervasive telephone snooping system called Echelon, and many other programs. There are good reasons to understand the ramifications of the many technological advancements we have seen over the century to make sure that the good technology is not used by the government to do bad things.

The 20th Century has truly been a century of unbelievable technological advancement. We should be cognizant of what this technology has done to the size and nature of our own government. It could easily be argued that, with greater technological advances, the need for government ought to decline and private alternatives be enhanced. But there's not much evidence for that argument. In 1902 the cost of government activities at all levels came to 7.7% of the GDP; today it's more than 50%.

Government officials oversee everything we do from regulating the amount of water in our commodes to placing airbags in our cars, safety locks on our guns, and using our own land. Almost every daily activity we engage in is monitored or regulated by some government agency. If one attempts to just avoid government harassment, one finds himself in deep trouble with the law.

Yes, we can be grateful that the technological developments in the marketplace over the last 100 years have made our lives more prosperous and enjoyable, but any observant person must be annoyed by the ever-present "Big Brother" that watches and records our every move. The idea that we're responsible for our own actions has been seriously undermined. And it would be grossly misleading to argue that the huge growth in the size of government has been helpful and necessary in raising the standard of living of so many Americans. Since government cannot create anything, it can only resort to using force to redistribute the goods that energetic citizens produce. The old-fashioned term for this is "theft." It's clear that our great prosperity has come in spite of the obstacles that big government places in our way and not because of it. And besides, our current prosperity may well not be as permanent as many believe.

Quite a few major changes in public policy have occurred in this century. These changes in policy reflect our current attitude toward the American Republic and the Constitution and help us to understand what to expect in the future. Economic prosperity seems to have prevailed, but the appropriate question asked by too few Americans is, "Have our personal liberties been undermined?"

Taxes are certainly higher. A federal income tax of 35 to 40% is something many middle-class Americans must pay, while on average they work for the government for more than half the year. In passing on our estates from one generation to the next, our "partner," the US government, decides on its share before the next generation can take over. The estate tax certainly verifies the saying about the inevitability of death and taxes. At the turn of the century we had neither, and in spite of a continuous outcry against both, there's no sign that either will soon be eliminated.

Accepting the principle behind both the income and the estate tax concedes the statist notion that the government owns the fruits of our labor, as well as our savings, and we are permitted by the politicians' "generosity" to keep a certain percentage. Every tax-cut proposal in Washington now is considered a "cost" to government, not the return of something rightfully belonging to a productive citizen. This principle is true whether it's a 1% or a 70% income tax. Concern for this principle has been rarely expressed in a serious manner over the past 50 years. The withholding process has permitted many to believe that a tax rebate at the end of the year comes as a gift from government. Because of this, the real cost of government to the taxpayer is obscured. The income tax has grown to such an extent and the government is so dependent on it that any talk of eliminating the income tax is just that, talk.

A casual acceptance of the principle behind high taxation, with an income tax and an inheritance tax, is incompatible with a principled belief in a true Republic. It is impossible to maintain a high tax system without the sacrifice of liberty and an undermining of property ownership. If kept in place, such a system will undermine prosperity, regardless of how well off we may presently be.

In truth, the amount of taxes we now pay compared to 100 years ago is shocking. There is little philosophic condemnation by the intellectual community, the political leaders, or the media of this immoral system. This should be a warning sign to all of us that, even in less prosperous times, we can expect high taxes and that our productive economic system will come under attack. Not only have we seen little resistance to the current high tax system, it has become an acceptable notion that this system is moral and is a justified requirement to finance the welfare/warfare state. Propaganda polls are continuously cited claiming that the American people don't want tax reductions. High taxes, except for only short periods of time, are incompatible with liberty and prosperity.

We will, I'm sure, be given the opportunity in the early part of this next century to make a choice between the two. I am certain of my preference.

There was no welfare state in 1900. In the year 2000 we have a huge welfare state, which continues to grow each year. Not that special-interest legislation didn't exist in the 19th Century, but for the most part, it was limited and directed toward moneyed interests--the most egregious example being the railroads.

The modern-day welfare state has steadily grown since the Great Depression of the 1930s. The federal government is now involved in providing health care, houses, unemployment benefits, education, food stamps to millions, plus all kinds of subsidies to every conceivable special-interest group. Welfare is now part of our culture, costing hundreds of billions of dollars every year. It is now thought to be a "right," something one is "entitled" to. Calling it an "entitlement" makes it sound proper and respectable and not based on theft. Anyone who has a need, desire, or demand and can get the politicians' attention will get what he wants, even though it may be at the expense of someone else. Today it is considered morally right and politically correct to promote the welfare state. Any suggestion otherwise is considered political suicide.

The acceptance of the welfare ethic and rejection of the work ethic as the accepted process for improving one's economic conditions are now ingrained in our political institutions. This process was started in earnest in the 1930s, received a big boost in the 1960s, and has continued a steady growth, even through the 1990s, despite some rhetoric in opposition. This public acceptance has occurred in spite of the fact that there is no evidence that welfare is a true help in assisting the needy. Its abject failure around the world where welfarism took the next step into socialism has even a worse record.

The transition in the past hundred years from essentially no welfare to an all-encompassing welfare state represents a major change in attitude in the United States. Along with its acceptance, the promoters have dramatically reinterpreted the Constitution from the way it had been for our first 150 years. Where the general welfare clause once had a clear general meaning (which was intended to prohibit special-interest welfare, and was something they detested and revolted against under King George), it is now used to justify any demand of any group, as long as a majority in Congress votes for it.

But the history is clear and the words in the Constitution are precise. Madison and Jefferson in explaining the general welfare clause left no doubt as to its meaning.

Madison said: "With respect to the words 'general welfare,' I have always regarded them as qualified by the detail of power connected with them. To take them in a literal and unlimited sense would be a metamorphosis of the Constitution into a character which there is a host of proofs not contemplated by its creators." Madison argued that there would be no purpose whatsoever for the enumeration of the particular powers if the general welfare clause was to be broadly interpreted. The Constitution granted authority to the federal government to do only 20 things, each to be carried out for the benefit of the general welfare of all the people. This understanding of the Constitution, as described by the Father of the Constitution, has been lost in this century.

Jefferson was just as clear, writing in 1798, when he said: "Congress has not unlimited powers to provide for the general welfare but only those specifically enumerated."

With the modern-day interpretation of the general welfare clause, the principle of individual liberty and the doctrine of enumerated powers have been made meaningless. The goal of strictly limiting the power of our national government as was intended by the Constitution is impossible to achieve as long as it is acceptable for Congress to redistribute wealth in an egalitarian welfare state. There's no way that personal liberty will not suffer with every effort to expand or make the welfare state efficient. And the sad part is that the sincere efforts to help people do better economically through welfare programs always fail. Dependency replaces self-reliance while the sense of self worth of the recipient suffers, making for an angry, unhappy, and dissatisfied society. The cost in dollar terms is high, but the cost in terms of liberty is even greater, but generally ignored, and in the long run, there's nothing to show for this sacrifice.

Today, there's no serious effort to challenge welfare as a way of life, and its uncontrolled growth in the next economic downturn is to be expected. Too many citizens now believe they are "entitled" to monetary assistance from the government anytime they need it, and they expect it. Even in times of plenty, the direction has been to continue expanding education, welfare, and retirement benefits. No one asks where the government gets the money to finance the welfare state. Is it morally right to do so? Is it authorized in the Constitution? Does it help anyone in the long run? Who suffers from the policy? Until these questions are seriously asked and correctly answered, we cannot expect the march toward a pervasive welfare state to stop, and we can expect our liberties to be continuously compromised.

The concept of the Doctrine of Enumerated Powers was picked away at in the latter part of the 19th Century over strong objection by many constitutionalists. But it was not until the drumbeat of fear coming from the Roosevelt administration, during the Great Depression, that the courts virtually rewrote the Constitution by a reinterpretation of the general welfare clause. In 1936 the New Deal Supreme Court told Congress and the American people that the Constitution is irrelevant when it comes to limits being placed on congressional spending. In a ruling justifying the Agricultural Adjustment Act, the Court pronounced: "The power of Congress to authorize appropriations of public money for public purposes is not limited by the grants of legislative power found in the Constitution." With the stroke of a pen, the courts amended the Constitution in such a sweeping manner that it literally legalized the entire welfare state, which not surprisingly, has grown by leaps and bounds ever since. Since this ruling, we have rarely heard the true explanation of the general welfare clause as being a restriction of government power, not a grant of unlimited power.

We cannot ignore corporate welfare, which is part of the problem. Most people think the welfare state involves only giving something to the unfortunate poor. This is generally true, but once the principle is established that special benefits are legitimate the moneyed interests see the advantages in influencing the legislative process. Our system, which pays lip service to free enterprise and private-property ownership, is drifting toward a form of fascism or corporatism, rather than conventional socialism. And where the poor never seem to benefit under welfare, corporations become richer.

But it should have been expected that once the principle of favoritism was established, the contest would be over who has the greatest clout in Washington. No wonder lobbyists are willing to spend $125 million per month influencing Congress! It's a good investment. No amount of campaign finance reform or regulation of lobbyists can deal with this problem.

The problem lies in the now-accepted role for our government. Government has too much control over people and the market, making the temptation and incentive to influence government irresistible and to a degree necessary. Curtailing how people spend their own money or their right to petition their government will do nothing to help this influence peddling. Treating the symptoms and not the disease only further undermines the principles of freedom and property ownership.

Any serious reforms or effort to break away from the welfare state must be directed as much at corporate welfare as routine welfare. Since there's no serious effort to reject welfare on principle, the real conflict over how to divide what government plunders will continue. Once it's clear that the nation is not nearly as wealthy as it appears, this will become a serious problem, and it will get the attention it deserves.

Preserving liberty and restoring constitutional precepts are impossible as long as the welfare mentality prevails, and that will not likely change until we've run out of money. But it will become clear, as we move into the next century, that perpetual wealth and the so-called balanced budget, along with an expanding welfare state, cannot continue indefinitely. Any effort to perpetuate it will only occur with the further erosion of liberty.

The role of the US government in public education has changed dramatically over the past 100 years. Most of the major changes have occurred in the second half of this century. In the 19th century, the closest the federal government got to public education was the Land Grant College program. In the last 40 years, the federal government has essentially taken charge of the entire system. It is involved in education at every level through loans, grants, court directives, regulations, and curriculum manipulation. In 1900 it was of no concern to the federal government how local schools were run at any level.

After hundreds of billions of dollars, we have yet to see a shred of evidence that the drift toward central control over education has helped. By all measurements, the quality of education is down. There are more drugs and violence in the public schools than ever before. Discipline is impossible out of fear of lawsuits or charges of civil rights violations.

Controlled curricula have downplayed the importance of our constitutional heritage while indoctrinating our children, even in kindergarten, with environmental mythology, internationalism, and sexual liberation. Neighborhood schools in the early part of the 20th Century did not experience this kind of propaganda.

The one good result coming from our failed educational system has been the limited but important revival of the notion that parents are responsible for their children's education, not the state. We have seen literally millions of children taken from the public school system and taught at home or in private institutions in spite of the additional expense. This has helped many students and has also served to pressure the government schools into doing a better job. And the statistics show that middle-income and low-income families are the most eager to seek an alternative to the public school system.

There is no doubt that the way schools are run, how the teachers teach, and how the bills are paid is dramatically different from 100 years ago. And even though some that go through public schools do exceptionally well, there is clear evidence that the average high school graduate today is far less educated than his counterpart was in the early part of this century.

Due to the poor preparation of our high school graduates, colleges expect very little from their students, since nearly everyone gets to go to college who wants to. Public school is compulsory and college is available to almost everyone regardless of qualifications. In 1914, English composition was required in 98% of our college; today it's about one-third. Only 12% of today's colleges require mathematics be taught, where in 1914, 82% did. No college now requires literature courses. But, rest assured plenty of social-babble courses are required as we continue to dumb down our nation.

Federal funding for education grows every year, hitting $38 billion this year, $1 billion more than requested by the administration and 7% over last year. Great congressional debates occur over the size of a classroom, student and teacher testing, bilingual education, teacher's salaries, school violence, and drug usage. And it's politically incorrect to point out that all these problems are not present in the private schools. Every year there is less effort at the federal level to return education to the people, the parents, and the local school officials. For 20 years at least, some of our Presidential candidates advocated abolishing the Department of Education and for the federal government to get completely out of the public education business. This year we will hear no more of that. The President got more money for education than he asked for, and it's considered not only bad manners but also political suicide to argue the case for stopping all federal government education programs. Talk of returning some control of federal programs to the state is not the same as keeping the federal government out of education as directed by the Constitution.

Of the 20 congressionally authorized functions granted by the Constitution, education is not one of them. That should be enough of a reason not to be involved, but there's no evidence of any benefit, and statistics show that great harm has resulted. It has cost us hundreds of billions of dollars, yet we continue the inexorable march toward total domination of our educational system by Washington bureaucrats and politicians. It makes no sense!

It's argued that if the federal funding for education did not continue education would suffer even more. Yet we see poor and middle-class families educating their children at home or at a private school at a fraction of the cost of a government school education, with results fantastically better--and all done in the absence of violence and drugs. A case can be made that there would be more money available for education if we just left the money in the states to begin with and never brought it to Washington for the bureaucrats and the politicians to waste. But it looks like Congress will not soon learn this lesson, so the process will continue and the results will get worse.

The best thing we could do now is pass a bill to give parents a $3,000 tax credit for each child they educate. This would encourage competition and allow a lot more choice for parents struggling to help their children get a decent education.

The practice of medicine is now a government-managed care system, and very few Americans are happy with it. Not only is there little effort to extricate the federal government from the medical-care business, but the process of expanding the government's role continues unabated. At the turn of the 19th Century, it was not even considered a possibility that medical care was the responsibility of the federal government. Since Lyndon Johnson's Great Society programs of the 1960s, the role of the federal government in delivering medical care has grown exponentially. Today the federal government pays more than 60% of all the medical bills and regulates all of it. The demands continue for more free care at the same time complaints about the shortcomings of managed care multiply. Yet it's natural to assume that government planning and financing will sacrifice quality care. It is now accepted that people who need care are entitled to it as a right. This is a serious error in judgment.

There's no indication that the trend toward government medicine will be reversed. Our problems are related to the direct takeover of medical care in programs like Medicare and Medicaid. But it's also been the interference in the free market through ERISA mandates related to HMOs and other managed-care organizations, as well as our tax code, that have undermined the private insurance aspect of paying for medical care. True medical insurance is not available. The government dictates all the terms.

In the early stages patients, doctors, and hospitals welcomed these programs. Generous care was available with more than adequate reimbursement. It led to what one would expect: abuse, overcharges, and overuse. When costs rose, it was necessary through government rulemaking and bureaucratic management to cut reimbursement and limit the procedures available and personal choice of physicians. We don't have socialized medicine, but we do have bureaucratic medicine, mismanaged by the government and select corporations who usurped the decision-making power from the physician. The way medical care is delivered today in the United States is a perfect example of the evils of corporatism, an artificial system that only politicians responding to the special interests could create.

There's no reason to believe the market cannot deliver medical care in as efficient a manner as it does computers, automobiles, and televisions. But the confidence is gone and everyone assumes, just as it is in education, that only a federal bureaucracy is capable of solving the problems of maximizing the number of people, including the poor, who receive the best medical care available. In an effort to help the poor, the quality of care has gone down for everyone else and the costs have skyrocketed.

Making generous medical savings accounts available is about the only program talked about today that offers an alternative to government mismanaged care. If something of this sort is not soon implemented, we can expect more pervasive government involvement in the practice of medicine. With a continual deterioration of its quality, the private practice of medicine will soon be gone.

Government housing programs are no more successful than the federal government's medical and education programs. In the early part of this century, government housing was virtually unheard of. Now the HUD budget commands over $30 billion each year and increases every year. Finances of mortgages through the Federal Home Loan Bank, the largest federal government borrower, is the key financial institution pumping in hundreds of billions of dollars of credit into the housing market, making things worse. The Federal Reserve has now started to use home mortgage securities for monetizing debt.

Public housing has a reputation for being a refuge for drugs, crimes, and filth, with projects being torn down as routinely as they are built. There's every indication that this entitlement will continue to expand in size, regardless of its failures. Token local control over these expenditures will do nothing to solve the problem. Recently the Secretary of HUD, using public funds to sue gun manufacturers, claimed this is necessary to solve the problem of crime which government housing perpetuates. If a government agency, which was never meant to exist in the first place under the Constitution, can expand their role into legislative and legal matters without the consent of Congress, we indeed have a serious problem on our hands. The programs are bad enough in themselves, but the abuse of the rule of law and ignoring the separation of powers makes these expanding programs that much more dangerous to our entire political system and is a direct attack on personal liberty.

If one cares about providing the maximum and best housing for the maximum number of people, one must consider a free-market approach in association with a sound non-depreciating currency. We have been operating a public housing program directly opposite to this, and along with steady inflation and government promotion of housing since the 1960s, the housing market has been grossly distorted. We can soon expect a major downward correction in the housing industry, prompted by rising interest rates.

Our attitudes toward foreign policy have dramatically changed since the beginning of the century. From George Washington through Grover Cleveland, the accepted policy was to avoid entangling alliances. Although we spread our wings westward and southward as part of our manifest destiny, in the 19th Century we accepted the Monroe Doctrine notion that Europeans and Asians should stay out of our affairs in this hemisphere and we theirs. McKinley, Teddy Roosevelt, and the Spanish American War changed all of that. Our intellectual and political leaders at the turn of the last century brought into vogue the interventionist doctrine setting the stage for the past 100 years of global military activism.

From a country that once minded its own business, we now find ourselves with military personnel in more than 130 different countries, protecting our modern-day American empire. Not only do we have troops spread to the four corners of the earth, we find Coast Guard Cutters in the Mediterranean and around the world, our FBI in any country we choose, and the CIA in places the Congress doesn't even know about.

It is a truism that the state grows and freedom is diminished in times of war. Almost perpetual war in the 20th Century has significantly contributed to steadily undermining our liberties while glorifying the state. In addition to the military wars, liberty has also suffered from the domestic "wars" on poverty, literacy, drugs, homelessness, privacy, and many others.

We have, in the last 100 years, gone from the accepted and cherished notion of a sovereign nation to one of a globalist, New World Order. As we once had three separate branches of our government, the United Nations proudly uses its three branches, the World Bank, the IMF, and the World Trade Organization to work their will in this new era of globalism. Because the US is by far the strongest military industrial power, it can dictate the terms of these international institutions, protecting what we see as our various interests such as oil, along with satisfying our military industrial complex. Our commercial interests and foreign policy are no longer separate. This allows for subsidized profits, while the taxpayers are forced to protect huge corporations against any losses from overseas investments. The argument that we go about the world out of humanitarian concerns for those suffering-which was the excuse for bombing Serbia-is a farce.

As bad as it is that average Americans are forced to subsidize such a system, we additionally are placed in greater danger because of our arrogant policy of bombing nations that do not submit to our wishes. This generates the hatred directed toward America, even if at times it seems suppressed, and exposes us to a greater threat of terrorism, since this is the only vehicle our victims can use to retaliate against a powerful military state.

But even with the apparent success of our foreign policy and the military might we still have, the actual truth is that we have spread ourselves too thinly and may well have difficulty defending ourselves if we are ever threatened by any significant force around the world. At the close of this century, we find our military preparedness and morale at an all-time low. It will become more obvious as we move into the 21st Century that the cost of maintaining this worldwide presence is too high and cutbacks will be necessary. The cost in terms of liberties lost and the unnecessary exposure to terrorism are difficult to determine, but in time it will become apparent to all of us that foreign interventionism is of no benefit to American citizens, but instead is a threat to our liberties.

Throughout our early history and up to World War I, our wars were fought with volunteers. There was no military draft except for a failed attempt by Lincoln in the Civil War, which ended with justified riots and rebellion against it. The attitudes toward the draft definitely changed over the past century. Draftees were said to be necessary to fight in World War I, World

War II, Korea, and Vietnam. This change in attitude has definitely satisfied those who believe that we have an obligation to police the world. The idiocy of Vietnam served as a catalyst for an anti-draft attitude, which is still alive today. Fortunately, we have not had a draft for over 25 years, but Congress refuses to address this matter in a principled fashion by abolishing, once and for all, the useless Selective Service System. Too many authoritarians in Congress still believe that in times of need an army of teenage draftees will be needed to defend our commercial interests throughout the world..

A return to the spirit of the Republic would mean that a draft would never be used and all able-bodied persons would be willing to volunteer in defense of their liberty. Without the willingness to do so, liberty cannot be saved. A conscripted army can never substitute for the willingness of freedom-loving Americans to defend their country out of their love for liberty.

The US monetary system during the 20th Century has

dramatically changed from the one authorized by the Constitution. Only silver and gold were to be used in payment of debt and no paper money was to be issued. In one of the few restrictions on the states, the Constitution prohibited them from issuing their own money and they were to use only gold and silver in payment of debt. No central bank was authorized. The authors of the Constitution were well aware of the dangers of inflation, having seen the great harm associated with the destruction of the Continental currency. They never wanted to see another system that ended with the slogan "It's not worth a Continental." They much preferred "sound as a dollar" or "as good as gold" as a description of our currency. Unfortunately their concerns, as they were reflected in the Constitution, have been ignored and, as this century closes, we do not have a sound dollar "as good as gold." The changes to our monetary system are by far the most significant economic events of the 20th Century.

The gold dollar of 1900 is now nothing more than a Federal Reserve note with a promise by untrustworthy politicians and the central bankers to pay nothing for it. No longer is there silver or gold available to protect the value of a steadily depreciating currency. This is a fraud of the worst kind and the type of crime that would put a private citizen behind bars.

But there have been too many special interests benefiting by our fiat currency, too much ignorance and too much apathy regarding the nature of money. We will surely pay the price for this negligence. The relative soundness of our currency that we enjoy as we move into the 21st Century will not persist. The instability in world currency markets, because of the dollars' acceptance for so many years as a reserve currency, will cause devastating adjustments that Congress will eventually be forced to deal with.

The transition from sound money to paper money did not occur instantaneously. It occurred over a 58-year period between 1913 and 1971 and the mischief continues today. Our central bank, the Federal Reserve System (established in 1913 after two failed efforts in the

19th Century) has been the driving force behind the development of our current fiat system. Since the turn of the century, we have seen our dollar lose 95% of its purchasing power, and it continues to depreciate. This is nothing less than theft, and those responsible should be held accountable. The record of the Federal Reserve is abysmal. Yet at the close of the 20th Century, its chairman is held in extremely high esteem, with almost zero calls for study of the monetary system with intent to once again have the dollar linked to gold.

Ironically, the government and politicians are held in very low esteem, yet the significant trust in them to maintain the value of the currency is not questioned. But it should be.

The reasons for rejecting gold and promoting paper are not mysterious, since quite a few special interests benefit. Deficit financing is much more difficult when there's no central bank available to monetize government debt. This gives license to politicians to spend lavishly on the projects that are most likely to get them reelected. War is more difficult to pursue if government has to borrow or tax the people for its financing. The Federal Reserve's ability to create credit out of thin air to pay the bills run up by Congress, establishes a symbiosis that is easy for the politicians to love. It's also advantageous for the politicians to ignore the negative effects from such a monetary arrangement, since they tend to be hidden and disseminated.

A paper-money system attracts support from various economic groups. Bankers benefit from the "float" they get with a fractional reserve banking system that accompanies a fiat monetary system. Giant corporations, who get to borrow large funds at below-market interest rates, enjoy the system and consistently call for more inflation and artificially low interest rates. Even the general public seems to benefit from the artificial booms brought about by credit creation, with lower interest rates allowing major purchases like homes and cars.

The naïve and uninformed fully endorse the current system, because the benefits are readily apparent while the disadvantages are hidden, delayed, or not understood. The politicians, central bankers, commercial banks, big-business borrowers all believe their needs justify such a system. But the costs are many and the dangers are real. Because of easy credit throughout this century, we have found that financing war was easier than if taxes had to be raised. The many wars we have fought and the continuous military confrontations in smaller wars since Vietnam have made the 20th Century a bloody century. It is most likely that we would have pursued a less militaristic foreign policy if financing it had been more difficult. Likewise, financing the welfare state would have progressed much slower if our deficits could not have been financed by an accommodative central bank willing to inflate the money supply at will.

There are other real costs as well, that few are willing to believe are a direct consequence of Federal Reserve Board policy. Rampant inflation after World War I, as well as the 1921 Depression, were a consequence of monetary policy during and following the war. The stock market speculation of the 1920s, the stock market collapse of 1929, and the Depression of the 1930s (causing millions to be unemployed) all resulted from Federal Reserve Board monetary mischief.

Price inflation of the early 1950s was a consequence of monetary inflation required to fight the Korean War. Wage and price controls used then totally failed, yet the same canard was used during the Vietnam War in the early 1970s to again impose wage and price controls with even worse results. All the price inflation, all the distortions, all the recessions and unemployment should be laid at the doorstep of the Federal Reserve. The Fed is an accomplice in promoting all unnecessary war as well as the useless and harmful welfare programs with its willingness to cover Congress' profligate spending habits.

Even though the Fed did great harm before 1971, after the total elimination of the gold dollar linkage, the problems of deficit spending, welfare expansion, and military industrial complex influence have gotten much worse.

Although many claim the 1990s have been great economic years, Federal Reserve board action of the past decade has caused problems yet to manifest themselves. The inevitable correction will come as the new century begins and is likely to be quite serious.

The stage has been set. Rampant monetary growth has led to historic high asset inflation, massive speculation, over-capacity, malinvestment, excessive debt, negative savings rate, and a current account deficit of huge proportions. These conditions dictate a painful adjustment, something that would have never occurred under a gold standard. The special benefits of foreigners taking our inflated dollars for low-priced goods and then loaning them back to us will eventually end. The dollar must fall, interest rates must rise, price inflation will accelerate, the financial asset bubble will burst, and a dangerous downturn in the economy will follow. There are many reasons to believe the economic slowdown will be worldwide since the dollar is the reserve currency of the world. An illusion about our dollar's value has allowed us to prop up Europe and Japan in this past decade during a period of weak growth for them, but when reality sets in, economic conditions will deteriorate. Greater computer speed, which has helped to stimulate the boom of the 1990s, will work in the opposite direction as all the speculative positions unwind, and that includes the tens of trillion of dollars in derivatives. There was a good reason the Federal Reserve rushed in to rescue Long-Term Capital Management with a multi-billion dollar bailout. It was unadulterated fear that the big correction was about to begin. Up until now, feeding the credit bubble with even more credit has worked and is the only tool they have to fight the business cycle, but eventually control will be lost.

A paper money system is dangerous economically and not constitutionally authorized. It's also immoral for government to "counterfeit" money, which dilutes the value of the currency and steals value from those who hold the currency and those who did not necessarily benefit from its early circulation. Not everyone benefits from the largesse of government spending programs or a systematic debasement of the currency. The middle class, those not on welfare and not in the military industrial complex, suffer the most from rising prices and job losses in the correction phase of the business cycle. Congress must someday restore sound money to America. It's mandated in the Constitution; it's economically sound to do so; and it's morally right to guarantee a standard of value for the money. Our oath of office obligates all Members of Congress to pay attention to this and participate in this needed reform.

A police state is incompatible with liberty. A hundred years ago the federal government was responsible for enforcing very few laws. This has dramatically changed. There are now over 3,000 federal laws and 10,000 regulations employing hundreds of thousands of bureaucrats diligently enforcing them, with over 80,000 of them carrying guns. We now have an armed national police state, just as Jefferson complained of King George in the Declaration of Independence: "He has sent hither swarms of officers to harass our people and eat out their substance." A lot of political and police power has shifted from the state and local communities to the federal government over the past hundred years. If a constitutional republic is desired and individual liberty is cherished, this concentration of power cannot be tolerated.

Congress has been derelict in creating the agencies in the first place and ceding to the executive the power to write regulations and even tax without congressional approval. These agencies enforce their own laws and supervise their own administrative court system where citizens are considered guilty until proven innocent. The Constitution has been thrown out the window for all practical purposes, and although more Americans everyday complain loudly, Congress does nothing to stop it.

The promoters of bureaucratic legislation claim to

have good intentions but they fail to acknowledge the costs, the inefficiency or the undermining of individual rights. Worker safety, environmental concerns, drug usage, gun control, welfarism, banking regulations, government insurance, health programs, insurance against economic and natural disasters, and regulation of fish and wildlife are just a few of the issues that prompt the unlimited use of federal regulatory and legislative power to deal with perceived problems. But inevitably, for every attempt to solve one problem, government creates two new ones. National politicians aren't likely to volunteer a market or local-government solution to a problem, or they will find out how unnecessary they really are.

Congress' careless attitude about the federal bureaucracy and its penchant for incessant legislation have prompted serious abuse of every American citizen. Last year alone there were more than 42,000 civil forfeitures of property occurring without due process of law or a conviction of a crime, and oftentimes the owners weren't even charged with a crime. Return of illegally seized property is difficult, and the owner is forced to prove his innocence in order to retrieve it. Even though many innocent Americans have suffered, these laws have done nothing to stop drug usage or change people's attitudes toward the IRS. Seizures and forfeitures only make the problems they are trying to solve that much worse. The idea that a police department, under federal law, can seize property and receive direct benefit from it is an outrage. The proceeds can be distributed to the various police agencies without going through the budgetary process. This dangerous incentive must end.

The national police state mentality has essentially taken over crime investigation throughout the country. Our local sheriffs are intimidated and frequently overruled by the national police. Anything worse than writing traffic tickets prompts swarms of federal agents to the scene. We frequently see the FBI, DEA, CIA, BATF, Fish and Wildlife, IRS, federal marshals, and even the Army involved in local law enforcement. They don't come to assist, but to take over. The two most notorious examples of federal abuse of police powers were seen at Ruby Ridge and Waco, where non-aggressive citizens were needlessly provoked and killed by federal agents. At Waco even army tanks were used to deal with a situation the local sheriff could have easily handled. These two incidents are well known, but thousands of other similar abuses routinely occur with little publicity. The federal police-state, seen in action at Ruby Ridge and Waco, hopefully is not a sign of things to come; but it could be if we're not careful.

If the steady growth of the federal police power continues, the American Republic cannot survive. The Congresses of the 20th Century have steadily undermined the principle that the government closest to home must deal with law and order and not the federal government. The federal courts also have significantly contributed to this trend. Hopefully, in the new century, our support for a national police state will be diminished.

We have, in this past century, not only seen the undermining of the federalism that the Constitution desperately tried to preserve, but the principle of separations of power among the three branches of government has been severely compromised as well.

The Supreme Court no longer just rules on constitutionality but frequently rewrites the law with attempts at comprehensive social engineering. The most blatant example was the Roe vs. Wade ruling. The federal courts should be hearing a lot fewer cases, deferring as often as possible to the state courts. Throughout the 20th Century with Congress' obsession for writing laws for everything, the federal courts were quite willing to support the idea of a huge interventionist federal government. The fact that the police officers in the Rodney King case were tried twice for the same crime, ignoring the constitutional prohibition against double jeopardy, was astoundingly condoned by the courts rather than condemned. It is not an encouraging sign that the concept of equal protection under the law will prevail.

When it comes to Executive Orders, it's gotten completely out of hand. Executive Orders may legitimately be used by a President to carry out his constitutionally authorized duties but that would require far fewer orders than modern-day Presidents have issued. As the 20th Century comes to a close, we find the executive branch willfully and arrogantly using the Executive Order to deliberately circumvent the legislative body and bragging about it.

Although nearly 100,000 American battle deaths have occurred since World War II, and both big and small wars have been fought almost continuously, there has not been a congressional declaration of war since 1941. Our Presidents now fight wars, not only without explicit congressional approval, but also in the name of the United Nations with our troops now serving under foreign commanders. Our Presidents have assured us that UN authorization is all that's needed to send our troops into battle. The 1973 War Powers Resolution, meant to restrict Presidential war powers, has either been ignored by our Presidents or used to justify war for up to 90 days. The Congress and the people, too often, have chosen to ignore this problem saying little about the recent bombing in Serbia. The continual bombing of Iraq, which has now been going on for over 9 years, is virtually ignored. If a President can decide on the issue of war, without a vote of the Congress, a representative republic does not exist. Our Presidents should not have the authority to declare national emergencies, and they certainly should not have authority to declare marshal law, a power the Congress has already granted for any future emergency. Economic and political crises can develop quickly, and overly aggressive Presidents are only too willing to enhance their own power in dealing with them.

Congress, sadly, throughout this century has been only too willing to grant authority to our Presidents at the sacrifice of its own. The idea of separate but equal branches of government has been forgotten and the Congress bears much of the responsibility for this trend.

Executive Powers in the past hundred years, have grown steadily with the creation of agencies that write and enforce their own regulations and with Congress allowing the President to use Executive Orders without restraint. But in addition, there have been various other special vehicles that our Presidents use without congressional oversight. For example the Exchange Stabilization Fund, set up during the Depression, has over $34 billion available to be used at the President's discretion without congressional approval. This slush fund grows each year as it is paid interest on the securities it holds. It was instrumental in the $50 billion Mexican bailout in 1995.

The CIA is so secretive that even those Congressmen privy to its operation have little knowledge of what this secret government actually does around the world. We know, of course, it has been involved in the past 50 years in assassinations and government overthrows on frequent occasions.

The Federal Reserve operation, which works hand-in-hand with the administration, is not subject to congressional oversight. The Fed manipulates currency exchange rates, controls short-term interest rates, and fixes the gold price; all behind closed doors. Bailing out foreign governments, financial corporations, and huge banks can all be achieved without congressional approval. A hundred years ago when we had a gold standard, credit could not be created out of thin air, and because a much more limited government philosophy prevailed, this could not have been possible. Today it's hard to even document what goes on, let alone expect Congress to control it.

The people should be able to closely monitor the government, but as our government grows in size and scope, it seeks to monitor our every move. Attacks on our privacy are incessant and are always justified by citing so-called legitimate needs of the state, efficiency, and law enforcement. Plans are laid for numerous data banks to record everyone's activities. A national ID card using our social security number is the goal of many, and even though we achieved a significant victory in delaying its final approval last year, the promoters will surely persist in their efforts. Plans are made for a medical data bank to be kept and used against our wishes. Job banks and details of all our lending activities continue to be of interest to all national policing agencies to make sure they know exactly where the drug dealers, illegal aliens, and tax dodgers are and what they're doing, it is argued. For national security purposes, the Echelon system of monitoring all overseas phone calls has been introduced, yet the details of this program are not available to any inquiring Member of Congress.

The government knew very little about each individual American citizen in 1900, but starting with World War I, there has been a systematic growth of government surveillance of everyone's activities, with multiple records being kept. Today, true privacy is essentially a thing of the past. The FBI and the IRS have been used by various administrations to snoop and harass political opponents and there has been little effort by

Congress to end this abuse. A free society, that is a constitutional republic, cannot be maintained if privacy is not highly cherished and protected by the government, rather than abused by it.

And we can expect it to get worse. Secretary of Defense Bill Cohen was recently quoted as saying: "Terrorism is escalating to the point that US citizens may soon have to choose between civil liberties and more intrusive forms of protection;" all in the name of taking care of us! As far as I am concerned, we could all do with a lot less government protection and security. The offer of government benevolence is the worst reason to sacrifice liberty, but we have seen a lot of that during the 20th Century.

Probably the most significant change in attitude that occurred in the 20th Century was that with respect to life itself. Although abortion has been performed for hundreds if not thousands of years, it was rarely considered an acceptable and routine medical procedure without moral consequence. Since 1973 abortion in

America has become routine and justified by a contorted understanding of the right to privacy. The difference between American's rejection of abortions at the beginning of the century, compared to today's casual acceptance, is like night and day. Although a vocal number of Americans express their disgust with abortion on demand, our legislative bodies and the courts claim that the procedure is a constitutionally protected right, disregarding all scientific evidence and legal precedents that recognize the unborn as a legal living entity deserving protection of the law. Ironically the greatest proponents of abortion are the same ones who advocate imprisonment for anyone who disturbs the natural habitat of a toad.

This loss of respect for human life in the latter half of the 20th Century has yet to have its full impact on our society. Without a deep concern for life, and with the casual disposing of living human fetuses, respect for liberty is greatly diminished. This has allowed a subtle but real justification for those who commit violent acts against fellow human beings.

It should surprise no one that a teenager delivering a term newborn is capable of throwing the child away in a garbage dumpster. The new mother in this circumstance is acting consistently knowing that if an abortion is done just before a delivery it's legally justified and the abortionist is paid to kill the child. Sale of fetal parts to tax-supported institutions is now an accepted practice. This moral dilemma that our society has encountered over the past 40 years, if not resolved in favor of life, will make it impossible for a system of laws to protect the life and liberty of any citizen. We can expect senseless violence to continue as a sense of self-worth is undermined.

Children know that mothers and sisters when distraught have abortions to solve the problem of an unwanted pregnancy. Distraught teenagers in copying this behavior are now more prone to use violence against others or themselves when provoked or confused. This tendency is made worse because they see, in this age of abortion, their own lives as having less value, thus destroying their self-esteem.

The prime reason government is organized in a free society is to protect life-not to protect those who take life. Today, not only do we protect the abortionist, we take taxpayers funds to pay for abortions domestically as well as overseas. This egregious policy will continue to plague us well into the 21st Century.

A free society designed to protect life and liberty is incompatible with government sanctioning and financing abortion on demand. It should not be a surprise to anyone that as abortion became more acceptable, our society became more violent and less free. The irony is that Roe vs. Wade justified abortion using a privacy argument, conveniently forgetting that not protecting the innocent unborn is the most serious violation of privacy possible. If the location of the fetus is the justification for legalized killing, the privacy of our homes would permit the killing of the newborn, the deformed, and the elderly-a direction in which we find ourselves going. As government-financed medical care increases, we will hear more economic arguments for euthanasia-that's "mercy" killing for the benefit of the budget planners. Already we hear these economic arguments for killing the elderly and terminally ill.

Last year the House made a serious error by trying to federalize the crime of killing a fetus occurring in an act of violence. The stated goal was to emphasize that the fetus deserved legal protection under the law. And indeed it should and does-at the state level. Federalizing any act of violence is unconstitutional; essentially all violent acts should be dealt with by the states. And because we have allowed the courts and Congress to federalize such laws, we find more good state laws are overridden than good federal laws written. Roe vs. Wade federalized state abortion laws and ushered in the age of abortion. The Unborn Victims of Violence Act, if passed into law, will do great harm by explicitly excluding abortionists, thus codifying for the first time the Roe vs. Wade concept and giving even greater legal protection to the abortionist.

The responsibility of the Congress is twofold. First, we should never fund abortions. Nothing could be more heinous than forcing those with strong right-to-life beliefs to pay for abortions. Second, Roe vs. Wade must be replaced by limiting jurisdiction, which can be done through legislation-a constitutional option. If we as a nation do not once again show respect and protect the life of the unborn, we can expect the factions that have emerged on each side of this issue to become more vocal and violent. A nation that can casually toss away its smallest and most vulnerable members and call it a "right" cannot continue to protect the lives or rights of its other citizens.

Much has changed over the past hundred years. Where technology has improved our living standards, we find that our government has significantly changed from one of limited scope to that of pervasive intervention.

A hundred years ago, it was generally conceded that one extremely important government function was to enforce contracts made voluntarily in the marketplace. Today government notoriously interferes with almost every voluntary economic transaction. Consumerism, labor-law, wage standards, hiring and firing regulations, political correctness, affirmative action, the Americans with Disabilities Act, the tax code, and others all place a burden on the two parties struggling to transact business. The EPA, OSHA, and government-generated litigation also interfere with voluntary contracts. At times it seems a miracle that our society adapts and continues to perform reasonably well in spite of the many bureaucratic dictates.

As the 20th Century comes to a close, we see a dramatic change from a government that once served an important function by emphasizing the value of voluntary contracts to one that excessively interferes with them.

Although the interference is greater in economic associations than in social, the principle is the same. Already we see the political correctness movement interfering with social and religious associations. Data banks are set up to keep records on everyone, especially groups with strong religious views and anybody who would be so bold as to call himself a "patriot". The notion that there is a difference between murder and murder driven by hate has established the principle of thought crime, a dangerous trend indeed.

When the business cycle turns down, all the regulations and laws that interfere with economic and personal transactions will not be as well tolerated, and then the true cost will become apparent. It is under the conditions of a weak economy that such government interference generates a reaction to the anger over the rules that has been suppressed.

To the statist, the idea that average people can and should take care of themselves by making their own decisions, and that they don't need Big Brother to protect them in everything they do, is anathema to the way they think. The bureaucratic mindset is convinced that without the politicians' efforts, no one would be protected from anything, rejecting the idea of a free-market economy out of ignorance or arrogance.

This change in the 20th Century has significantly contributed to the dependency of our poor on government handouts, the recipients being convinced they are entitled to help and that they are incapable of taking care of themselves. A serious loss of self-esteem and unhappiness result, even if the system on the short run seems to help them get by.

There were no federal laws at the end of the 19th Century dealing with drugs or guns. Gun violence was rare, and abuse of addictive substances was only a minor problem. Now after a hundred years of progressive government intervention in dealing with guns and drugs, with thousands of laws and regulations, we have more gun violence and a huge drug problem. Before the social authoritarians decided to reform the gun and drug culture, they amended the Constitution enacting alcohol prohibition. Prohibition failed to reduce alcohol usage, and a crime wave resulted. After

14 years, the American people demanded repeal of this social engineering amendment and got it. Prohibition prompted the production of poor-quality alcohol with serious health consequences, while respect for the law was lost as it was fragrantly violated. At least at that time the American people believed the Constitution had to be amended to prohibit the use of alcohol, something that is ignored today in the federal government's effort to stop drug usage.In spite of the obvious failure of alcohol prohibition, the federal government after its repeal, turned its sights on gun ownership and drug usage.

The many federal anti-gun laws written since 1934, along with the constant threat of outright registration and confiscation, have put the FBI and the BATF at odds with millions of law-abiding citizens who believe the Constitution is explicit in granting the right of gun ownership to all non-violent Americans. Our government pursued alcohol prohibition in the 1920s and confiscation of gold in the 1930s, so it's logical to conclude that our government is quite capable of confiscating all privately owned firearms. That has not yet occurred, but as we move into the next century, many in Washington advocate just that and would do it if they didn't think the American people would revolt, just as they did against alcohol prohibition.

Throughout this century, there has been a move toward drug prohibition starting with the Harrison Act in 1912. The first federal marijuana law was pushed through by FDR in 1938, but the real war on drugs has been fought with intensity for the past 30 years.

Hundreds of billions of dollars have been spent, and not only is there no evidence of reduced drug usage, we have instead seen a tremendous increase. Many deaths have occurred from overdoses of street drugs, since there is no quality control or labeling. Crime, as a consequence of drug prohibition, has skyrocketed, and our prisons are overflowing. Many prisoners are non-violent and should be treated as patients with addictions, not as criminals. Irrational mandatory minimal sentences have caused a great deal of harm.

We have non-violent drug offenders doing life sentences, and there is no room to incarcerate the rapists and murderers.

With drugs and needles illegal, the unintended consequence of the spread of AIDs and hepatitis through dirty needles has put a greater burden on the taxpayers who are forced to care for the victims. This ridiculous system that offers a jail cell for a sick addict rather than treatment has pushed many a young girl into prostitution to pay for drugs priced hundreds of times higher than they are worth. But the drug dealers love the system and dread a new approach. When we finally decide that drug prohibition has been no more successful than alcohol prohibition, the drug dealers will disappear.

But the monster drug problem we have created is compounded by moves to tax citizens so government can hand out free needles to drug addicts who are breaking the law, in hopes there will be less spread of hepatitis and AIDs in order to reduce government health-care costs. This proposal shows how bankrupt we are at coming to grips with this problem.

And it seems we will never learn. Tobacco is about to be categorized as a drug and a prohibition of sorts imposed. This will make the drug war seem small if we continue to expand the tobacco war. Talk about insane government policies of the 20th Century, tobacco policy wins the prize. First we subsidize tobacco in response to demands by the special interests, knowing full well even from the beginning that tobacco had many negative health consequences. Then we spend taxpayers' money, warning the people of its dangers without stopping the subsidies. Government then pays for the care of those who choose to smoke despite the known dangers and warnings. But it did not stop there. The trial lawyers' lobby saw to it that local government entities could sue tobacco companies for reimbursements of the excess costs they were bearing in taking care of smoking-related illnesses. And the only way this could be paid for was to place a tax on those people who smoke.

How could such silliness go on for so long? For one reason. We as a nation have forgotten a basic precept of a free society-that all citizens must be responsible for their own acts. If one smokes and gets sick, that's the problem of the one making the decision to smoke, or take any other risks for that matter, not the innocent taxpayers who have already been forced to pay for the tobacco subsidies and government health warning ads. Beneficiaries of this monstrous policy have been: tobacco farmers, tobacco manufacturers, politicians, bureaucrats, smokers, health organizations and physicians, and especially the trial lawyers. Who suffers? The innocent taxpayers that have no voice in the matter and who acted responsibly and chose not to smoke. Think of what it would mean if we followed this same logic and implemented a federal social program, similar to the current war on smoking, designed to reduce the spread of AIDS within the gay community. Astoundingly, we have done the opposite by making AIDS a politically correct disease. There was certainly a different attitude a hundred years ago regarding those with sexually transmitted diseases like syphilis, compared to the special status given AIDS victims today.

And it is said an interventionist economy is needed to make society fair to everyone! We need no more government "fairness" campaigns. Egalitarianism never works and inevitably penalizes the innocent. Government in a free society is supposed to protect the innocent, encourage self-reliance, and impose equal justice while allowing everyone to benefit from their own effort and suffer the consequence of their acts.

A free and independent people need no authoritarian central government dictating eating, drinking, gambling, sexual or smoking habits. When rules are required, they should come from the government closest to home, as it once did prior to America's ill-fated 20th Century experiment with alcohol prohibition. Let's hope we show more common sense in the 21st Century in these matters than we did in the 20th.

A compulsive attitude by politicians to regulate non-violent behavior may be well intentioned but leads to many unintended consequences. Legislation passed in the second half of the 20th Century dealing with drugs and personal habits has been the driving force behind the unconstitutional seizure and forfeiture laws and the loss of financial privacy. The war on drugs is the most important driving force behind the national police state. The excuse given for calling in the Army helicopters and tanks at the Waco disaster was that the authorities had evidence of an amphetamine lab on the Davidian's property. This was never proven, but nevertheless it gave the legal cover-but not the proper constitutional authority-for escalating the attack on the Davidians, which led to the senseless killing of so many innocent people. The attitude surrounding this entire issue needs to change. We should never turn over the job of dealing with bad habits to our federal government. That is a recipe for disaster.

4. Social and Philosophic changes.

America has not only changed technologically in the past hundred years, but our social attitudes and personal philosophies have changed as well. We have less respect for life and less love for liberty. We are obsessed with material things, along with rowdy and raucous entertainment. Needs and wants have become rights for both rich and poor. The idea of instant gratification too often guides our actions, and when satisfaction is not forthcoming anger and violence break out. Road rage and airline passenger rage are seen more frequently. Regardless of fault, a bad outcome in almost anything, even if beyond human control will prompt a lawsuit. Too many believe they deserve to win the lottery, and a lawsuit helps the odds. Unfortunately the only winners too often are the lawyers hyping the litigation.

Few Americans are convinced anymore that productive effort is the most important factor in economic success and personal satisfaction. One did not get rich in the 1990s investing in companies that had significant or modest earnings. The most successful investors bought companies that had no earnings and the gambling paid off big. This attitude cannot create perpetual wealth and must someday end.

Today financial gurus are obsessed with speculation in the next initial public offering (IPO) and express no interest in the cause of liberty, without which markets cannot exist.

Lying and cheating are now acceptable by the majority. This was not true a hundred years ago when moral standards were higher. The October 1999 issue of US News and World Report reveals that 84% of college students believe cheating is necessary to get ahead in today's world, and 90% are convinced there's no price to pay for cheating. Not surprisingly, 90% of college students believe politicians often cheat. An equal percentage believe the media cheats as well. There's no way to know if the problem is this bad in the general population, but these statistics indicate our young people do not trust our politicians or media. Trust has been replaced with a satisfaction in the materialism that a speculative stock market, borrowing money, and a spendthrift government can generate. But what happens to our society if the material abundance, which we enjoy, is ephemeral and human trust is lost?

Social disorder will surely result and there will be a clamor for a more authoritarian government. This scenario may indeed threaten the stability of our social order and significantly undermine all our constitutional protections. But there is no law or ethics committee that will solve this problem of diminishing trust and honesty-that is a problem of the heart, mind, and character to be dealt with by each individual citizen. The importance of the family unit today has been greatly diminished compared to the close of the 19th Century. Now, fewer people get married, more divorces occur, and the number of children born out of wedlock continues to rise. Tax penalties are placed on married couples; illegitimacy and single parenthood are rewarded by government subsidies, and we find many authoritarians arguing that the definition of marriage should change in order to allow non-husband and wife couples to qualify for welfare handouts. The welfare system has mocked the concept of marriage in the name of political correctness, economic egalitarianism, and hetero-phobia.

Freedom of speech is still cherished in America, but the political correctness movement has seriously undermined dissent on our university campuses. A conservative or libertarian black intellectual is clearly not treated with the same respect afforded an authoritarian black spokesman. We now hear of individuals being sent to psychiatrists when personal and social views are rude or out of the ordinary. It was commonplace in the Soviet system to incarcerate political dissenters in "mental" institutions. Those who received a Soviet government designation of "socially undesirable elements" were stripped of their rights. Will this be the way we treat political dissent in the future? We hear of people losing their jobs because of "socially undesirable" thoughts or for telling off-color jokes. Today sensitivity courses are routinely required in America to mold social thinking for the simplest of infractions.

The thought-police are all around us. It's a bad sign.

Any academic discussion questioning the wisdom of our policies surrounding World War II is met with shrill accusations of anti-Semitism and Nazi lover. No one is even permitted without derision by the media, the university intellectuals, and the politicians to ask why the United States allied itself with the murdering Soviets and then turned over Eastern Europe to them while ushering in a 45-year saber-rattling dangerous cold war period. "Free speech" is permitted in our universities for those who do not threaten the status quo of welfarism, globalism, corporatism, and a financial system that provides great benefits to powerful special interests. If a university professor does not follow the party line, he does not receive tenure.

We find ourselves at the close of this century realizing all our standards have been undermined. A monetary standard for our money is gone; the dollar is whatever the government tells us it is. There is no definition, and no promise to pay anything for the notes issued ad infinitum by the government.

Standards for education are continually lowered, de-emphasizing excellence. Relative ethics are promoted, and moral absolutes are ridiculed. The influence of religion on our standards is frowned upon and replaced by secular humanistic standards.

The work ethic has been replaced by a welfare ethic, based on need not effort. Strict standards required for an elite military force are gone, and our lack of readiness reflects this.

Standards of behavior of our professional athletes seem to reflect the rules followed in the ring by the professional wrestlers where anything goes.

Managed medical care, driven by government decrees, has reduced its quality and virtually ruined the doctor-patient relationship.

Movie and TV standards are so low that our young

people's senses are totally numbed by them.

Standards of courtesy on highways, airplanes, and shops are seriously compromised and at time lead to senseless violence.

With the acceptance of abortion, our standards for life have become totally arbitrary as they have become for liberty. Endorsing the arbitrary use of force by our government morally justifies the direct use of force by disgruntled groups not satisfied with the slower government process.

The standards for honesty and truth have certainly deteriorated during the past hundred years.

Property ownership has been undermined through environmental regulations and excessive taxation. True ownership of property no longer exists.

There has been a systematic undermining of legal and constitutional principles once respected and followed for the protection of individual liberty.

A society cannot continue in a state of moral anarchy. Moral anarchy will lead to political anarchy. A society without clearly understood standards of conduct cannot remain stable any more than an architect can design and build a sturdy skyscraper with measuring instruments that change in value each day. We recently lost a NASA space probe because someone failed to convert inches to centimeters-a simple but deadly mistake in measuring physical standards. If we as a people debase our moral standards, the American Republic will meet a similar fate.

5. Law and Morality

Many Americans agree that this country is facing a moral crisis that has been especially manifested in the closing decade of the 20th Century. Our President's personal conduct, the characters of our politicians in general, the caliber of the arts, movies and television, and our legal system have reflected this crisis. The personal conduct of many of our professional athletes and movie stars has been less than praiseworthy.

Some politicians, sensing this, have pushed hard to write and strictly enforce numerous laws regarding personal non-violent behavior with the hope that the people will become more moral. This has not happened, but it has filled our prisons. This year it will cost more than $40 billion to run our prison system. The prison population, nearing 2 million, is up 70% in the last decade and two-thirds of all the inmates did not commit an act of violence. Mandatory minimum drug-sentencing laws have been instrumental in this trend.

Laws clearly cannot alter moral behavior, and if it is attempted, it creates bigger problems. Only individuals with moral convictions can make "society" moral. But the law does reflect the general consensus of the people regarding force and aggression, which is a moral issue. Government can be directed to restrain and punish violent aggressive citizens or it can use aggressive force to rule the people, redistribute wealth, make citizens follow certain moral standards, and force them to practice certain personal habits. Once government is permitted to do the latter, even in a limited sense, the guiding principle of an authoritarian government is established and its power and influence over the people will steadily grow at the expense of personal liberty.

No matter how well intentioned, an authoritarian government always abuses its powers. In its effort to achieve an egalitarian society, the principle of inequality that freedom recognizes and protects is lost. Government then, instead of being an obstacle to violence becomes the biggest perpetrator. This invites all the special interests to manipulate the monopoly and evil use of government power. Twenty thousand lobbyists currently swarm Washington seeking special advantage. That's where we find ourselves today.

Although government cannot and should not try to make people better in the personal moral sense, proper law should have a moral non-aggressive basis to it-no lying, cheating, stealing, killing, injuring, or threatening. Government then would be limited to protecting contracts, people, and property, while guaranteeing all personal non-violent behaviors-even the controversial.

Although there are degrees in various authoritarian societies as to how much power a government may wield, once government is given authority to wield power, it does so in an ever-increasing fashion. The pressure to use government authority to run the economy and our lives depends on several factors. These include a basic understanding of personal liberty, respect for a constitutional republic, economic myths, ignorance, and misplaced good intentions. In every society there are always those waiting in the wings for an opportunity to show how brilliant they are, as they lust for power, convinced they know what's best for everyone. But the defenders of liberty know that what is best for everyone is to be left alone, with a government limited to stopping aggressive behavior.

6. Philosophic Explanation

The 20th Century has produced socialist dictators the world over, from Stalin, Hitler and Mao to Pol Pot, Castro, and Ho Chi Minh. More than 200 million people died as a result of the bad ideas of these evil men. Each and every one of these dictators despised the principle of private-property ownership-which then undermined all the other liberties cherished by the people.

It is argued that the United States and now the world have learned of a Third Way-something between extreme socialism and mean-spirited capitalism. But this is a dream. The so-called friendly Third Way endorses 100% the principle that government authority can be used to direct our lives and the economy. Once this is accepted, the principle that man alone is responsible for his salvation and his life on earth, which serves as the foundation for free-market capitalism, is rejected. The Third Way of friendly welfarism, or soft fascism, that is, where government and businesses are seen as partners, undermines freedom and sets the stage for authoritarian socialism. Personal liberty cannot be preserved if we remain on the course on which we find ourselves at the close of the 20th Century.

In our early history, it was understood that a free society embraced both personal civil liberties and economic liberties. During the 20th Century, this unified concept of freedom has been undermined. Today we have one group talking about economic freedom while interfering with our personal liberty and the other group condemning economic liberty, while preaching the need to protect personal civil liberties. Both groups reject liberty 50% of the time. That leaves very few who defend liberty all the time. Sadly, there are too few in this country who today understand and defend liberty in both areas. A common debate that we hear occurs over how we can write laws protecting normal speech and at the same time limiting commercial speech as if they were two entirely different things.

Many Americans wonder why Congress pays so little attention to the Constitution and are bewildered as to how so much inappropriate legislation gets passed. But the Constitution is not entirely ignored. It is used correctly at times when it's convenient and satisfies a particular goal, but never consistently across the board on all legislation. And too, the Constitution is all too frequently made to say exactly what the authors of special legislation want it to say. That's the modern way; language can be made relative to our times. But without a precise understanding and respect for the supreme law of the land, i.e., the Constitution, it no longer serves as the guide for the rule of law. In its place we have substituted the rule of man and the special interests.

That's how we have arrived at the close of this century without a clear understanding or belief in the cardinal principles of the Constitution-the separation of powers and the principle of federalism. Instead, we are rushing toward a powerful executive, centralized control, and a Congress greatly diminished in importance. Executive Orders, agency regulations, federal court rulings, and unratified international agreements direct our government, economy, and foreign policy. Congress has truly been reduced in status and importance over the past hundred years. And when the people's voices are heard, it's done indirectly through polling, allowing our leaders to decide how far they can go without stirring up the people. But this is opposite to what the Constitution was supposed to do. It was meant to protect the rights of the minority from the dictates of the majority. The majority vote of the powerful and the influential was never meant to rule the people.

We may not have a king telling us which trees we can cut down, but we do have a government bureaucracy and a pervasive threat of litigation by radical environmentalists who keep us from cutting our own trees, digging a drainage ditch, or filling a puddle-all at the expense of private-property ownership.

The key element in a free society is that individuals should wield control of their own lives, receiving the benefits and suffering the consequences of all their acts. Once the individual becomes a pawn of the state, whether a monarch or a majority runs the state, a free society can no longer endure. We are dangerously close to that happening in America, even in the midst of plenty and with the appearance of contentment. If individual freedom is carelessly snuffed out, the creative energy needed for productive pursuits will dissipate. Government produces nothing, and in its effort to redistribute wealth, can only destroy it.

Freedom too often is rejected-especially in the midst of plenty--when there is a belief that government largesse will last forever. This is true because it is tough to accept personal responsibility, practice the work ethic, and follow the rules of peaceful co-existence with our fellow man. Continuous vigilance against the would-be tyrants who promise security at minimal cost must be maintained. The temptation is great to accept the notion that everyone can be a beneficiary of the caring state and a winner of the lottery or a class-action lawsuit. But history has proven there is never a shortage of authoritarians-benevolent, of course-quite willing to tell others how to live for their own good. A little sacrifice of personal liberty is a small price to pay for long-time security, it is too often reasoned.

7. Worth the Effort

I have good friends who are in basic agreement with my analysis of the current state of the American Republic, but argue it is a waste of time and effort to try and change the direction in which we are going. No one will listen, they argue, and besides the development of a strong centralized authoritarian government is too far along to reverse the trends of the 20th Century. Why waste time in Congress when so few people care about liberty, they ask. The masses, they point out, are interested only in being taken care of, and the elite want to keep receiving the special benefits allotted to them through special-interest legislation.

I understand the odds, and I am not naïve enough to believe the effort to preserve liberty is a cakewalk. And I am very much aware of my own limitations in achieving this goal. But ideas, based on sound and moral principles, do have consequences. And powerful ideas can have major consequences beyond our wildest dreams. Our Founders clearly understood this, and they knew they would be successful, even against the overwhelming odds they faced. They described this steady confidence they shared with each other when hopes were dim as "divine providence." Good ideas can have good results and we must remember bad ideas can have bad results.

It is crucial to understand that vague and confusing idealism produces mediocre results, especially when it is up against a determined effort to promote an authoritarian system that is sold to the people as conciliatory and non-confrontational--a compromise, they say, between the two extremes. But it must be remembered that no matter how it's portrayed, when big government systematically and steadily undermines individual rights and economic liberty, it's still a powerful but negative idea and it will not fade away easily. Ideas of liberty are a great threat to those who enjoy planning the economy and running other people's lives.

The good news is that our numbers are growing. More Americans than ever before are very much aware of what's going on in Washington and how, on a daily basis, their liberties are being undermined. There are more intellectual think tanks than ever before promoting the market economy, private property ownership, and personal liberty. The large majority of Americans are sick and tired of being overtaxed and despise the income tax and the inheritance tax. The majority of Americans know government programs fail to achieve their goals and waste huge sums of money. A smoldering resentment against the unfairness of government efforts to force equality on us can inspire violence, but instead it should be used to encourage an honest system of equal justice based on individual not collective rights. Sentiment is moving in the direction of challenging the status quo of the welfare and international warfare state. The Internet has given hope to millions who have felt their voices were not being heard. And this influence is just beginning. The three major networks and conventional government propaganda no longer control the information now available to anyone with a computer.

The only way the supporters of big government can stop the Internet will be to tax, regulate, and monitor it, and although it is a major undertaking, plans are already being laid to do precisely that. Big government proponents are anxious to make the tax on the Internet an international tax as advocated by the United Nations, apply the Eschelon principle used to monitor all overseas phone calls to the Internet and prevent the development of private encryption that would guarantee privacy on the Internet. These battles have just begun, and if the civil libertarians and free-market proponents don't win this fight to keep the Internet free and private, the tools for undermining authoritarian government will be greatly reduced. Victory for liberty will probably elude us for decades. The excuse they will give for controlling the Internet will be to stop pornography, catch drug dealers, monitor child molesters, and to do many other "good" things. We should not be deceived.

We face tough odds, but to avoid battle or believe there is a place to escape to someplace else in the world would concede victory to those who endorse authoritarian government. The grand experiment in human liberty must not be abandoned. A renewed hope and understanding of liberty is what we need as we move into the 21st Century.

A perfectly free society we know cannot be achieved, and the idea of perfect socialism is an oxymoron. Pursuing that goal throughout the 20th Century has already caused untold human suffering. The clear goal of a free society must be understood and sought or the vision of the authoritarians will face little resistance and will easily fill the void.

There are precise goals Congress should work for, even under today's difficult circumstances. It must preserve, in the best manner possible, voluntary options to failed government programs. We must legalize freedom to the maximum extent possible.

1. Complete police protection is impossible; therefore we must preserve the right to own weapons in self-defense.

2. In order to maintain economic protection against government debasement of the currency, gold ownership must be preserved-something taken away from the American people during the Depression.

3. Adequate retirement protection by the government is limited, if not ultimately impossible. We must allow every citizen the opportunity to control all his or her retirement funds.

4. Government education has clearly failed. We must guarantee the right of families to home school or send

their kids to private schools and help them with tax credits.

5. Government snooping must be stopped. We must work to protect all our privacy, especially on the Internet, prevent the National ID Card, and to stop the development of all government data banks.

6. Federal police functions are unconstitutional and increasingly abusive. We should disarm all federal bureaucrats and return the police function to local authorities.

7. The army was never meant to be used in local policing activities. We must firmly prohibit our Presidents from using the military in local law enforcement operations which is now being planned for under the guise of fighting terrorism.

8. Foreign military intervention by our Presidents in recent years, to police the American Empire, is a costly failure. Foreign military intervention should not be

permitted without explicit congressional approval.

9. Competitions in all elections should be guaranteed, and the monopoly powers gained by the two major parties through unfair signature requirements, high fees, and campaign donation controls should be removed. Competitive parties should be allowed in all government sponsored debates.

10. We must do whatever is possible to help instill a spiritual love for freedom and recognize that our liberties depend on responsible individuals, not the group or the collective or society as a whole. The individual is the building block of a free and prosperous social order.

The Founders knew full well that the concept of liberty was fragile and could easily be undermined. They worried about the dangers that lay ahead. As we move into the new century, it is an appropriate time to rethink the principles upon which a free society rests.

Jefferson, concerned about the future, wrote: "Yes, we did produce a near-perfect republic. But will they keep it? Or will they, in the enjoyment of plenty, lose the memory of freedom? Material abundance without character is the path of destruction." "They" that he refers to are " we." And the future is now. Freedom, Jefferson knew, would produce "plenty," and with "material abundance" it's easy to forget the responsibility the citizens of a free society must assume if freedom and prosperity are to continue. The key element for the Republic's survival for Jefferson was the "character" of the people, something no set of laws can instill. The question today is not that of abundance, but of character, respect for others, their liberty and their property. It is the character of the people that determines the proper role for government in a free society.

Samuel Adams, likewise, warned future generations. He referred to "good manners" as the vital ingredient a free society needs to survive. Adams said: "Neither the wisest Constitution nor the wisest laws will secure the liberty and happiness of a people whose manners are universally corrupt."

The message is clear, if we lose our love of liberty and our manners become corrupt, character is lost and so is the Republic.

But character is determined by free will and personal choice by each of us individually. Character can be restored or cast aside at a whim. The choice is ours alone and our leaders should show the way.

Some who are every bit as concerned as I am about our future and the pervasive corrupt influence in our government in every aspect of our lives offer other solutions. Some say to solve the problem all we have to do is write more detailed laws dealing with campaign finance reform, ignoring how this might undermine the principles of liberty. Similarly, others argue that what is needed is merely to place tighter restrictions on the lobbyists in order to minimize their influence, but they fail to recognize that this undermines our constitutional right to petition our government for redress of grievances.

And there are others with equally good intentions that insist on writing even more laws and regulations punishing non-violent behavior in order to teach good manners and instill character. But they fail to see that tolerating non-violent behavior-even when stupid and dangerous to one's own self-is the same as our freedom to express unpopular political and offensive ideas and to promote and practice religion in any way one chooses. Resorting to writing more laws with the intent of instilling "character" and good "manners" in the people is anathema to liberty. The love of liberty can come only from within and is dependent on a stable family and a society that seeks the brotherhood of man through voluntary and charitable means.

And there are others who believe that government force is legitimate in promoting what they call fair economic redistribution. The proponents of this course have failed to read history and instead adhere to economic myths. They ignore the evidence that this effort to help their fellow man will inevitably fail. Instead, it will do the opposite and lead to the impoverishment of many more. But more importantly, if left unchecked this approach will destroy liberty by undermining the concept of private property ownership and free markets, the bedrock of economic prosperity.

None of these alternatives will work. Character and good manners are not a government problem. They reflect individual attitudes that can only be changed by individuals themselves. Freedom allows virtue and excellence to blossom. When government takes on the role of promoting virtue, illegitimate government force is used, and tyrants quickly appear on the scene to do the job. Virtue and excellence become illusive, and we find instead that the government officials become corrupt and freedom is lost-the very ingredient required for promoting virtue, harmony and the brotherhood of man.

Let's hope and pray that our political focus will soon

shift toward preserving liberty and individual responsibility and away from authoritarianism. The future of the American Republic depends on it. Let us not forget the American dream depends on keeping alive the spirit of liberty.

Cong. Rec. 16 May, 2000: H81-H87.

Monetary Policy

In 2007 the US Government reported that inflation for the previous year was 2.3 percent, the lowest figure in a decade. The average American consumer knows better. The Consumer Price Index is based off durable goods, and leaves out so called "volatile" commodities such as food, gasoline, and electricity. While its true that these commodities can fluctuate month to month, a consistent increase over multiple years, such as we have experienced, is not a volatile fluctuation.

As Ron Paul describes, this inflation is due to the irresponsible management of our currency by the Federal Reserve. The repeated cycles of boom and bust created by our mismanaged fiat currency have improved the fortunes of those on Wall St, but overall the average American has accumulated massive debt in an effort to keep up. Wage growth figures are skewed by the obscene decadence of hedge fund managers and their ilk. Inflation figures, which are used to determine Social Security payment increases, are judged by the cost of television sets and refrigerators, not the electricity that runs them, or the food that is stored in them. We are awash in good news about the economy, while the cost of food for the lower 75% of the population has increased 26%, while their wages have decreased 3%.

China is propping our economy up for now. We benefit from the years of growth in the value of the dollar, and we benefit from all international oil transactions being priced in dollars. The dollar is, for the moment, the reserve currency of most of the central banks and investment institutions of the world. However, as we continue to devalue our currency to maintain the relaxed lending environment that has allowed our cycle of boom and bust, the prospects for long term maintenance of this position become less and less secure. China will only sell our own dollars back to us for so long. If they were to dump all of their dollar denominated assets onto the world market today, the dollar would crash, and we would be faced with an economic downturn which would be comparable to the depression of the 1930's.

Notice the progression in the following speeches. The first is from 2000, before the collapse of the tech bubble and the crisis created by 9/11. Ron Paul has been consistent in his critiscism of the handling of US monetary policy in good times and in bad. Only now, as things are reaching the breaking point have people begun to really listen.

MANIPULATING INTEREST RATES

A speech by Ron Paul in the US House of

Representatives on May 15, 2000

The national debt is rising at an annual rate of a $100 billion per year while the federal government obligation to future generations is rising even faster. Yet, little concern is shown in Congress as our budgets grow and new programs are added on to old. Ordinary political deception has been replaced with the dangerous notion of invincibleness as members claim credit for imaginary budgetary surpluses. The percent of our income that government now takes continues to rise, while personal liberty is steadily compromised with each new budget. But the political euphoria associated with the "New Era" economy will soon come to an end.

Although many have done well during the last seven years of economic growth, many middle-income families have had to struggle just to keep up. For them, inflation is not dead and the easy fortunes made on Wall Street are as far removed as winning the lottery. When the economy enters into recession, this sense of frustration will spread.

Business cycles are well understood. They are not a natural consequence of capitalism but instead result from central bank manipulation of credit. This is especially true when the monetary unit is undefinable as it is in a fiat monetary system, such as ours. Therefore, it is correct to place blame on the Federal Reserve for all depressions/recessions, inflation, and much of the unemployment since 1913. The next downturn, likewise, will be the fault of the Fed.

It is true that the apparent prosperity and the boom

part of the cycle are a result of the Federal Reserve credit creation, but the price that must always be paid and the unfairness of inflationism makes it a dangerous process.

The silly notion that money can be created at will by a printing press or through computer entries is eagerly accepted by the majority as an easy road to riches, while ignoring any need for austerity, hard work, saving, and a truly free market economy. Those who actively endorse this system equate money creation with wealth creation and see it as a panacea for the inherent political difficulty in raising taxes or cutting spending.

A central bank that has no restraints placed on it is always available to the politicians who spend endlessly for reelection purposes. When the private sector lacks its appetite to lend sufficiently to the government, the Federal Reserve is always available to buy treasury debt with credit created out of thin air. At the slightest hint that interest rates are higher than the Fed wants, its purchase of debt keeps interest rates in check; that is, they are kept lower than the market rate. Setting interest rates is an enormous undertaking. It's price fixing and totally foreign to the principles of free market competition.

Since this process is economically stimulating, the politicians, the recipients of government largess, the bankers, and almost everyone enjoys the benefits of what seems to be a gift without cost.

But that's a fallacy. There is always a cost. Artificially low interest rates prompt lower savings, over-capacity expansion, mal-investment, excessive borrowing, speculation, and price increases in various segments of the economy. And since money creation is not wealth creation, it inevitably leads to a lower value for the currency. The inflation always comes to an end with various victims, many of whom never enjoyed the benefits of the credit creation and deficit spending.

This silly notion of money and credit gives rise to the conventional wisdom that once the economy gets really rolling, it's time for the Fed to stop economic growth. The false supposition is that economic growth causes higher prices and higher labor costs, and these evils must be prevented by tightening credit and raising interest rates. But these are only the consequences of the previous monetary expansion and blaming rising prices or higher labor costs is done only to distract from the real culprit-monetary inflation by the Federal Reserve.

In a free market, economic growth would never be considered a negative and purposely discouraged. It is strange that so many established economists and politicians accept the notion of dampening economic growth for this purpose. Economic growth with sound money always lowers prices-it never raises them. Deliberately increasing rates actually increase the cost of all borrowing, and yet it's claimed that this is necessary to stop rising costs. Obviously, there's not much to the soundness of central economic planning through monetary policy of this sort.

There are some who see this fallacy and object to deliberately slowing the economy but instead clamor for even more monetary growth to keep interest rates low and the economy booming. But this is just as silly because that leads to even more debasement of the currency, rising prices, and instead of lowering interest rates will in time, due to inflationary expectation, actually raise rates.

Fine-tuning the economy, through monetary manipulation is a dangerous game to play. We are now completing nearly a decade of rapid monetary growth and evidence is now appearing indicating that we will soon start to pay for our profligate ways. The financial bubble that the Fed manufactured over the past decade or two will burst and the illusion of our great wealth will end. In time, also the illusion of "surpluses for as far as the eye can see" will end. Then the Congress will be forced to take much more seriously the budgetary problems that it pretends do not exist.

Cong. Rec. 15 May, 2000: H3034.

The Dollar and Our Current Account Deficit

A speech by Ron Paul in the US House of

Representatives on June 6, 2007.

Fiat money, that is, money created out of thin air, causes numerous problems, internationally as well as domestic. It causes domestic price inflation, economic downturns, unemployment, excessive debt, (corporate, personal and government) mal-investment, and over capacity--all very serious and poorly understood by our officials. But fluctuating values of various paper currencies cause all kinds of disruptions in international trade and finance as well.

Trade surpluses and deficits when sound money conditions exist are of little concern since they prompt changes in policy or price adjustments in a natural or smooth manner. When currencies are non-convertible into something of real value, they can be arbitrarily increased at will, trade deficits and especially current account deficits are of much greater significance.

When trade imbalances are not corrected, sudden devaluations, higher interest rates, and domestic inflation are forced on the country that has most abused its monetary power. This was seen in 1997 in the Asian crisis, and precarious economic conditions continue in that region.

Japan has yet to recover from its monetary inflation of the 70s and 80s and has now suffered with a lethargic economy for over a decade. Even after this length of time there is no serious thought for currency reform in Japan or any other Asian nation.

Although international trade imbalances are a predictable result of fiat money, the duration and intensity of the cycles associated with it are not. A reserve currency, such as is the dollar, is treated by the market quite differently than another fiat currency.

The issuer of a reserve currency-in the case the United States-has greater latitude for inflating and can tolerate a current account deficit for much longer periods of time than other countries not enjoying the same benefit. But economic law, although at times it may seem lax, is ruthless in always demanding that economic imbalances arising from abuse of economic principles be rectified. In spite of the benefits that reserve currency countries enjoy, financial bubbles still occur and their prolongation, for whatever reason, only means the inevitable adjustment, when it comes, is more harsh.

Our current state of imbalance includes a huge US/foreign debt of $1.5 trillion, a record 20% of GDP and is a consequence of our continuously running a huge monthly current account deficit that shows no signs of soon abating. We are now the world's greatest debtor. The consequence of this deficit cannot be avoided. Our current account deficit has continued longer than many would have expected. But not knowing how long and to what extent deficits can go is not unusual. The precise event that starts the reversal in the trade balance is also unpredictable. The reversal itself is not.

Japan's lethargy, the Asian crisis, the Mexican financial crisis, Europe's weakness, the uncertainty surrounding the EURO, the demise of the Soviet system, and the ineptness of the Russian bailout, all contributed to the continued strength in the dollar and prolongation of our current account deficit. This current account deficit, which prompts foreigners to loan back dollars to us and to invest in our stock and bond markets, has contributed significantly to the financial bubble. The perception that the United States is the economic and military powerhouse of the world, helps perpetuate an illusion that the dollar is invincible and has encouraged our inflationary policies.

By inflating our currency, we can then spend our dollars overseas getting products at good prices which on the short run raises our standard of living - but, on borrowed money. All currency account deficits must be financed by borrowing from abroad.

It all ends when the world wakes up and realizes it has

been had by the US printing press. No country can expect to inflate its currency at will forever.

Since cartels never work, OPEC does not deserve credit for getting oil prices above $30 per barrel. Demand for equivalent purchasing power for the sale of oil, can. Recent commodity and wage price increases signal accelerating price inflation is at hand. We are witnessing the early stages in a sea change regarding the dollar, inflation, the stock market as well as commodity prices.

The nervousness in the stock and bond markets, and especially in the NASDAQ, indicates that the Congress may soon be facing an entirely different set of financial numbers regarding spending, revenues, interest costs on our national debt and the value of the US dollar. Price inflation of the conventional type will surely return, even if the economy slows.

Fiscal policy, and current monetary policy will not solve the crisis we will soon face. Only sound money, money that cannot be created out of thin air, can solve the many problems appearing on the horizon. The sooner we pay attention to monetary policy as the source of our international financial problems, the sooner we will come up with a sound solution.

Cong. Rec. 16 May, 2000: H3150.

What the Price of Gold is Telling Us

A speech by Ron Paul in the US House of

Representatives on April 25, 2006.

The financial press, and even the network news shows, have begun reporting the price of gold regularly. For twenty years, between 1980 and 2000, the price of gold was rarely mentioned. There was little interest, and the price was either falling or remaining steady.

Since 2001 however, interest in gold has soared along with its price. With the price now over $600 an ounce, a lot more people are becoming interested in gold as an investment and an economic indicator. Much can be learned by understanding what the rising dollar price of gold means.

The rise in gold prices from $250 per ounce in 2001 to over $600 today has drawn investors and speculators into the precious metals market. Though many already have made handsome profits, buying gold per se should not be touted as a good investment. After all, gold earns no interest and its quality never changes. It's static, and does not grow as sound investments should.

It's more accurate to say that one might invest in a gold or silver mining company, where management, labor costs, and the nature of new discoveries all play a vital role in determining the quality of the investment and the profits made.

Buying gold and holding it is somewhat analogous to converting one's savings into one hundred dollar bills and hiding them under the mattress-- yet not exactly the same. Both gold and dollars are considered money, and holding money does not qualify as an investment. There's a big difference between the two however, since by holding paper money one loses purchasing power. The purchasing power of commodity money, i.e. gold, however, goes up if the government devalues the circulating fiat currency.

Holding gold is protection or insurance against government's proclivity to debase its currency. The purchasing power of gold goes up not because it's a so-called good investment; it goes up in value only because the paper currency goes down in value. In our current situation, that means the dollar.

One of the characteristics of commodity money-- one that originated naturally in the marketplace-- is that it must serve as a store of value. Gold and silver meet that test-- paper does not. Because of this profound difference, the incentive and wisdom of holding emergency funds in the form of gold becomes attractive when the official currency is being devalued. It's more attractive than trying to save wealth in the form of a fiat currency, even when earning some nominal interest. The lack of earned interest on gold is not a problem once people realize the purchasing power of their currency is declining faster than the interest rates they might earn. The purchasing power of gold can rise even faster than increases in the cost of living.

The point is that most who buy gold do so to protect against a depreciating currency rather than as an investment in the classical sense. Americans understand this less than citizens of other countries; some nations have suffered from severe monetary inflation that literally led to the destruction of their national currency. Though our inflation-- i.e. the depreciation of the U.S. dollar-- has been insidious, average Americans are unaware of how this occurs. For instance, few Americans know nor seem concerned that the 1913 pre-Federal Reserve dollar is now worth only four cents. Officially, our central bankers and our politicians express no fear that the course on which we are set is fraught with great danger to our economy and our political system. The belief that money created out of thin air can work economic miracles, if only properly "managed," is pervasive in D.C.

In many ways we shouldn't be surprised about this trust in such an unsound system. For at least four generations our government-run universities have systematically preached a monetary doctrine justifying the so-called wisdom of paper money over the "foolishness" of sound money. Not only that, paper money has worked surprisingly well in the past 35 years-- the years the world has accepted pure paper money as currency. Alan Greenspan bragged that central bankers in these several decades have gained the knowledge necessary to make paper money respond as if it were gold. This removes the problem of obtaining gold to back currency, and hence frees politicians from the rigid discipline a gold standard imposes.

Many central bankers in the last 15 years became so confident they had achieved this milestone that they sold off large hoards of their gold reserves. At other times they tried to prove that paper works better than gold by artificially propping up the dollar by suppressing market gold prices. This recent deception failed just as it did in the 1960s, when our government tried to hold gold artificially low at $35 an ounce. But since they could not truly repeal the economic laws regarding money, just as many central bankers sold, others bought. It's fascinating that the European central banks sold gold while Asian central banks bought it over the last several years.

Since gold has proven to be the real money of the ages, we see once again a shift in wealth from the West to the East, just as we saw a loss of our industrial base in the same direction. Though Treasury officials deny any U.S. sales or loans of our official gold holdings, no audits are permitted so no one can be certain.

The special nature of the dollar as the reserve currency of the world has allowed this game to last longer than it would have otherwise. But the fact that gold has gone from $252 per ounce to over $600 means there is concern about the future of the dollar. The higher the price for gold, the greater the concern for the dollar. Instead of dwelling on the dollar price of gold, we should be talking about the depreciation of the dollar.

In 1934 a dollar was worth $1/20^{th}$ of an ounce of gold; $20 bought an ounce of gold. Today a dollar is worth $1/600^{th}$ of an ounce of gold, meaning it takes $600 to buy one ounce of gold.

The number of dollars created by the Federal Reserve, and through the fractional reserve banking system, is crucial in determining how the market assesses the relationship of the dollar and gold. Though there's a strong correlation, it's not instantaneous or perfectly predictable. There are many variables to consider, but in the long term the dollar price of gold represents past inflation of the money supply. Equally important, it represents the anticipation of how much new money will be created in the future. This introduces the factor of trust and confidence in our monetary authorities and our politicians. And these days the American people are casting a vote of "no confidence" in this regard, and for good reasons.

The incentive for central bankers to create new money out of thin air is twofold. One is to practice central economic planning through the manipulation of interest rates. The second is to monetize the escalating federal debt politicians create and thrive on.

Today no one in Washington believes for a minute that runaway deficits are going to be curtailed. In March alone, the federal government created an historic $85 billion deficit. The current supplemental bill going through Congress has grown from $92 billion to over $106 billion, and everyone knows it will not draw

President Bush's first veto. Most knowledgeable people therefore assume that inflation of the money supply is not only going to continue, but accelerate. This anticipation, plus the fact that many new dollars have been created over the past 15 years that have not yet been fully discounted, guarantees the further depreciation of the dollar in terms of gold.

There's no single measurement that reveals what the Fed has done in the recent past or tells us exactly what it's about to do in the future. Forget about the lip service given to transparency by new Fed Chairman Bernanke. Not only is this administration one of the most secretive across the board in our history, the current Fed firmly supports denying the most important measurement of current monetary policy to Congress, the financial community, and the American public. Because of a lack of interest and poor understanding of monetary policy, Congress has expressed essentially no concern about the significant change in reporting statistics on the money supply.

Beginning in March, though planned before Bernanke arrived at the Fed, the central bank discontinued compiling and reporting the monetary aggregate known as M3. M3 is the best description of how quickly the Fed is creating new money and credit. Common sense tells us that a government central bank creating new money out of thin air depreciates the value of each dollar in circulation. Yet this report is no longer available to us and Congress makes no demands to receive it.

Though M3 is the most helpful statistic to track Fed activity, it by no means tells us everything we need to know about trends in monetary policy. Total bank credit, still available to us, gives us indirect information reflecting the Fed's inflationary policies. But ultimately the markets will figure out exactly what the Fed is up to, and then individuals, financial institutions, governments, and other central bankers will act accordingly. The fact that our money supply is rising significantly cannot be hidden from the markets.

The response in time will drive the dollar down, while driving interest rates and commodity prices up. Already we see this trend developing, which surely will accelerate in the not too distant future. Part of this reaction will be from those who seek a haven to protect their wealth-- not invest-- by treating gold and silver as universal and historic money. This means holding fewer dollars that are decreasing in value while holding gold as it increases in value.

A soaring gold price is a vote of "no confidence" in the central bank and the dollar. This certainly was the case in 1979 and 1980. Today, gold prices reflect a growing restlessness with the increasing money supply, our budgetary and trade deficits, our unfunded liabilities, and the inability of Congress and the administration to reign in runaway spending.

Denying us statistical information, manipulating interest rates, and artificially trying to keep gold prices in check won't help in the long run. If the markets are fooled short term, it only means the adjustments will be much more dramatic later on. And in the meantime, other market imbalances develop.

The Fed tries to keep the consumer spending spree going, not through hard work and savings, but by creating artificial wealth in stock markets bubbles and housing bubbles. When these distortions run their course and are discovered, the corrections will be quite painful.

Likewise, a fiat monetary system encourages speculation and unsound borrowing. As problems develop, scapegoats are sought and frequently found in foreign nations. This prompts many to demand altering exchange rates and protectionist measures. The sentiment for this type of solution is growing each day.

Though everyone decries inflation, trade imbalances, economic downturns, and federal deficits, few attempt a closer study of our monetary system and how these events are interrelated. Even if it were recognized that a gold standard without monetary inflation would be advantageous, few in Washington would accept the political disadvantages of living with the discipline of gold-- since it serves as a check on government size and power. This is a sad commentary on the politics of today. The best analogy to our affinity for government spending, borrowing, and inflating is that of a drug addict who knows if he doesn't quit he'll die; yet he can't quit because of the heavy price required to overcome the dependency. The right choice is very difficult, but remaining addicted to drugs guarantees the death of the patient, while our addiction to deficit spending, debt, and inflation guarantees the collapse of our economy.

Special interest groups, who vigorously compete for federal dollars, want to perpetuate the system rather than admit to a dangerous addiction. Those who champion welfare for the poor, entitlements for the middle class, or war contracts for the military industrial corporations, all agree on the so-called benefits bestowed by the Fed's power to counterfeit fiat money. Bankers, who benefit from our fractional reserve system, likewise never criticize the Fed, especially since it's the lender of last resort that bails out financial institutions when crises arise. And it's true, special interests and bankers do benefit from the Fed, and may well get bailed out-- just as we saw with the Long-Term Capital Management fund crisis a few years ago. In the past, companies like Lockheed and Chrysler benefited as well. But what the Fed cannot do is guarantee the market will maintain trust in the worthiness of the dollar. Current policy guarantees that the integrity of the dollar will be undermined. Exactly when this will occur, and the extent of the resulting damage to financial system, cannot be known for sure-- but it is coming. There are plenty of indications already on the horizon.

Foreign policy plays a significant role in the economy and the value of the dollar. A foreign policy of militarism and empire building cannot be supported through direct taxation. The American people would never tolerate the taxes required to pay immediately for overseas wars, under the discipline of a gold standard. Borrowing and creating new money is much more politically palatable. It hides and delays the real costs of war, and the people are lulled into complacency-- especially since the wars we fight are couched in terms of patriotism, spreading the ideas of freedom, and stamping out terrorism. Unnecessary wars and fiat currencies go hand-in-hand, while a gold standard encourages a sensible foreign policy.

The cost of war is enormously detrimental; it significantly contributes to the economic instability of the nation by boosting spending, deficits, and inflation. Funds used for war are funds that could have remained in the productive economy to raise the standard of living of Americans now unemployed, underemployed, or barely living on the margin.

Yet even these costs may be preferable to paying for war with huge tax increases. This is because although fiat dollars are theoretically worthless, value is imbued by the trust placed in them by the world's financial community. Subjective trust in a currency can override objective knowledge about government policies, but only for a limited time.

Economic strength and military power contribute to the trust in a currency; in today's world trust in the U.S. dollar is not earned and therefore fragile. The history of the dollar, being as good as gold up until 1971, is helpful in maintaining an artificially higher value for the dollar than deserved.

Foreign policy contributes to the crisis when the spending to maintain our worldwide military commitments becomes prohibitive, and inflationary pressures accelerate. But the real crisis hits when the world realizes the king has no clothes, in that the dollar has no backing, and we face a military setback even greater than we already are experiencing in Iraq. Our token friends may quickly transform into vocal enemies once the attack on the dollar begins.

False trust placed in the dollar once was helpful to us, but panic and rejection of the dollar will develop into a real financial crisis. Then we will have no other option but to tighten our belts, go back to work, stop borrowing, start saving, and rebuild our industrial base, while adjusting to a lower standard of living for most Americans.

Counterfeiting the nation's money is a serious offense. The founders were especially adamant about avoiding the chaos, inflation, and destruction associated with the Continental dollar. That's why the Constitution is clear that only gold and silver should be legal tender in the United States. In 1792 the Coinage Act authorized the death penalty for any private citizen who counterfeited the currency. Too bad they weren't explicit that counterfeiting by government officials is just as detrimental to the economy and the value of the dollar.

In wartime, many nations actually operated counterfeiting programs to undermine our dollar, but never to a disastrous level. The enemy knew how harmful excessive creation of new money could be to the dollar and our economy. But it seems we never learned the dangers of creating new money out of thin air. We don't need an Arab nation or the Chinese to undermine our system with a counterfeiting operation. We do it ourselves, with all the disadvantages that would occur if others did it to us. Today we hear threats from some Arab, Muslim, and far Eastern countries about undermining the dollar system- not by dishonest counterfeiting, but by initiating an alternative monetary system based on gold. Wouldn't that be ironic? Such an event theoretically could do great harm to us. This day may well come, not so much as a direct political attack on the dollar system but out of necessity to restore confidence in money once again.

Historically, paper money never has lasted for long periods of time, while gold has survived thousands of years of attacks by political interests and big government. In time, the world once again will restore trust in the monetary system by making some currency as good as gold.

Gold, or any acceptable market commodity money, is required to preserve liberty. Monopoly control by government of a system that creates fiat money out of thin air guarantees the loss of liberty. No matter how well-intended our militarism is portrayed, or how happily the promises of wonderful programs for the poor are promoted, inflating the money supply to pay these bills makes government bigger. Empires always fail, and expenses always exceed projections. Harmful unintended consequences are the rule, not the exception. Welfare for the poor is inefficient and wasteful. The beneficiaries are rarely the poor themselves, but instead the politicians, bureaucrats, or the wealthy. The same is true of all foreign aid-- it's nothing more than a program that steals from the poor in a rich country and gives to the rich leaders of a poor country. Whether it's war or welfare payments, it always means higher taxes, inflation, and debt. Whether it's the extraction of wealth from the productive economy, the distortion of the market by interest rate manipulation, or spending for war and welfare, it can't happen without infringing upon personal liberty.

At home the war on poverty, terrorism, drugs, or foreign rulers provides an opportunity for authoritarians to rise to power, individuals who think nothing of violating the people's rights to privacy and freedom of speech. They believe their role is to protect the secrecy of government, rather than protect the privacy of citizens. Unfortunately, that is the atmosphere under which we live today, with essentially no respect for the Bill of Rights.

Though great economic harm comes from a government monopoly fiat monetary system, the loss of liberty associated with it is equally troubling. Just as empires are self-limiting in terms of money and manpower, so too is a monetary system based on illusion and fraud. When the end comes we will be given an opportunity to choose once again between honest money and liberty on one hand; chaos, poverty, and authoritarianism on the other.

The economic harm done by a fiat monetary system is pervasive, dangerous, and unfair. Though runaway inflation is injurious to almost everyone, it is more insidious for certain groups. Once inflation is recognized as a tax, it becomes clear the tax is regressive: penalizing the poor and middle class more than the rich and politically privileged. Price inflation, a consequence of inflating the money supply by the central bank, hits poor and marginal workers first and foremost. It especially penalizes savers, retirees, those on fixed incomes, and anyone who trusts government promises. Small businesses and individual enterprises suffer more than the financial elite, who borrow large sums before the money loses value. Those who are on the receiving end of government contracts--especially in the military industrial complex during wartime-- receive undeserved benefits.

It's a mistake to blame high gasoline and oil prices on price gouging. If we impose new taxes or fix prices, while ignoring monetary inflation, corporate subsidies, and excessive regulations, shortages will result. The market is the only way to determine the best price for any commodity. The law of supply and demand cannot be repealed. The real problems arise when government planners give subsidies to energy companies and favor one form of energy over another.

Energy prices are rising for many reasons: Inflation; increased demand from China and India; decreased supply resulting from our invasion of Iraq; anticipated disruption of supply as we push regime change in Iran; regulatory restrictions on gasoline production; government interference in the free market development of alternative fuels; and subsidies to big oil such as free leases and grants for research and development.

Interestingly, the cost of oil and gas is actually much higher than we pay at the retail level. Much of the DOD budget is spent protecting "our" oil supplies, and if such spending is factored in gasoline probably costs us more than $5 a gallon. The sad irony is that this military effort to secure cheap oil supplies inevitably backfires, and actually curtails supplies and boosts prices at the pump. The waste and fraud in issuing contracts to large corporations for work in Iraq only add to price increases.

When problems arise under conditions that exist today, it's a serious error to blame the little bit of the free market that still functions. Last summer the market worked efficiently after Katrina-- gas hit $3 a gallon, but soon supplies increased, usage went down, and the price returned to $2. In the 1980s, market forces took oil from $40 per barrel to $10 per barrel, and no one cried for the oil companies that went bankrupt. Today's increases are for the reasons mentioned above. It's natural for labor to seek its highest wage, and businesses to strive for the greatest profit. That's the way the market works. When the free market is allowed to work, it's the consumer who ultimately determines price and quality, with labor and business accommodating consumer choices. Once this process is distorted by government, prices rise excessively, labor costs and profits are negatively affected, and problems emerge. Instead of fixing the problem, politicians and demagogues respond by demanding windfall profits taxes and price controls, while never questioning how previous government interference caused the whole mess in the first place. Never let it be said that higher oil prices and profits cause inflation; inflation of the money supply causes higher prices!

Since keeping interest rates below market levels is synonymous with new money creation by the Fed, the resulting business cycle, higher cost of living, and job losses all can be laid at the doorstep of the Fed. This burden hits the poor the most, making Fed taxation by inflation the worst of all regressive taxes. Statistics about revenues generated by the income tax are grossly misleading; in reality much harm is done by our welfare/warfare system supposedly designed to help the poor and tax the rich. Only sound money can rectify the blatant injustice of this destructive system.

The Founders understood this great danger, and voted overwhelmingly to reject "emitting bills of credit," the term they used for paper or fiat money. It's too bad the knowledge and advice of our founders, and their mandate in the Constitution, are ignored today at our great peril. The current surge in gold prices-- which reflects our dollar's devaluation-- is warning us to pay closer attention to our fiscal, monetary, entitlement, and foreign policy.

A recent headline in the financial press announced that gold prices surged over concern that confrontation with Iran will further push oil prices higher. This may well reflect the current situation, but higher gold prices mainly reflect monetary expansion by the Federal Reserve. Dwelling on current events and their effect on gold prices reflects concern for symptoms rather than an understanding of the actual cause of these price increases. Without an enormous increase in the money supply over the past 35 years and a worldwide paper monetary system, this increase in the price of gold would not have occurred.

Certainly geo-political events in the Middle East under a gold standard would not alter its price, though they could affect the supply of oil and cause oil prices to rise. Only under conditions created by excessive paper money would one expect all or most prices to rise. This is a mere reflection of the devaluation of the dollar.

Particular things to remember:

If one endorses small government and maximum liberty, one must support commodity money.

One of the strongest restraints against unnecessary war is a gold standard.

Deficit financing by government is severely restricted by sound money.

The harmful effects of the business cycle are virtually eliminated with an honest gold standard.

Saving and thrift are encouraged by a gold standard; and discouraged by paper money.

Price inflation, with generally rising price levels, is

characteristic of paper money. Reports that the consumer price index and the producer price index are
rising are distractions: the real cause of inflation is the
Fed's creation of new money.

Interest rate manipulation by central bank helps the
rich, the banks, the government, and the politicians.

Paper money permits the regressive inflation tax to be
passed off on the poor and the middle class.

Speculative financial bubbles are characteristic of
paper money-- not gold.

Paper money encourages economic and political
chaos, which subsequently causes a search for scapegoats rather than blaming the central bank.

Dangerous protectionist measures frequently are
implemented to compensate for the dislocations

caused by fiat money.

Paper money, inflation, and the conditions they create contribute to the problems of illegal immigration.

The value of gold is remarkably stable.

The dollar price of gold reflects dollar   depreciation.

Holding gold helps preserve and store wealth, but technically gold is not a true investment.

Since 2001 the dollar has been devalued by 60%.

In 1934 FDR devalued the dollar by 41%.

In 1971 Nixon devalued the dollar by 7.9%.

In 1973 Nixon devalued the dollar by 10%.

These were momentous monetary events, and every knowledgeable person worldwide paid close attention. Major changes were endured in 1979 and 1980 to save the dollar from disintegration. This involved a severe recession, interest rates over 21%, and general price inflation of 15%.

Today we face a 60% devaluation and counting, yet no one seems to care. It's of greater significance than the three events mentioned above. And yet the one measurement that best reflects the degree of inflation, the Fed and our government deny us. Since March, M3 reporting has been discontinued. For starters, I'd like to see Congress demand that this report be resumed. I fully believe the American people and Congress are entitled to this information. Will we one day complain about false intelligence, as we have with the Iraq war? Will we complain about not having enough information to address monetary policy after it's too late?

If ever there was a time to get a handle on what sound money is and what it means, that time is today.

Inflation, as exposed by high gold prices, transfers wealth from the middle class to the rich, as real wages decline while the salaries of CEOs, movie stars, and athletes skyrocket-- along with the profits of the military industrial complex, the oil industry, and other special interests.

A sharply rising gold price is a vote of "no confidence" in Congress' ability to control the budget, the Fed's ability to control the money supply, and the administration's ability to bring stability to the Middle East.

Ultimately, the gold price is a measurement of trust in the currency and the politicians who run the country. It's been that way for a long time, and is not about to change.

If we care about the financial system, the tax system, and the monumental debt we're accumulating, we must start talking about the benefits and discipline that come only with a commodity standard of money-- money the government and central banks absolutely cannot create out of thin air.

Economic law dictates reform at some point. But should we wait until the dollar is 1/1,000 of an ounce of gold or 1/2,000 of an ounce of gold? The longer we wait, the more people suffer and the more difficult reforms become. Runaway inflation inevitably leads to political chaos, something numerous countries have suffered throughout the 20th century. The worst example of course was the German inflation of the 1920s that led to the rise of Hitler. Even the communist takeover of China was associated with runaway inflation brought on by Chinese Nationalists. The time for action is now, and it is up to the American people and the U.S. Congress to demand it.

Cong. Rec. 25 April 2006: H1729-H1733.

"Monetary Policy and the
State of the Economy"

Statement for Hearing before the House Financial Services Committee

Transparency in monetary policy is a goal we should all support. I've often wondered why Congress so willingly has given up its prerogative over monetary policy. Astonishingly, Congress in essence has ceded total control over the value of our money to a secretive central   bank.

Congress created the Federal Reserve, yet it had no constitutional authority to do so. We forget that those powers not explicitly granted to Congress by the Constitution are inherently denied to Congress-- and thus the authority to establish a central bank never was given. Of course Jefferson and Hamilton had that debate early on, a debate seemingly settled in 1913.

But transparency and oversight are something else, and they're worth considering. Congress, although not by law, essentially has given up all its oversight responsibility over the Federal Reserve. There are no true audits, and Congress knows nothing of the conversations, plans, and actions taken in concert with other central banks. We get less and less information regarding the money supply each year, especially now that M3 is no longer reported.

The role the Fed plays in the President's secretive Working Group on Financial Markets goes unnoticed by members of Congress. The Federal Reserve shows no willingness to inform Congress voluntarily about how often the Working Group meets, what actions it takes that affect the financial markets, or why it takes those actions.

But these actions, directed by the Federal Reserve, alter the purchasing power of our money. And that purchasing power is always reduced. The dollar today is worth only four cents compared to the dollar in 1913, when the Federal Reserve started. This has profound consequences for our economy and our political stability. All paper currencies are vulnerable to collapse, and history is replete with examples of great suffering caused by such collapses, especially to a nation's poor and middle class. This leads to political turmoil.

Even before a currency collapse occurs, the damage done by a fiat system is significant. Our monetary system insidiously transfers wealth from the poor and middle class to the privileged rich. Wages never keep up with the profits of Wall Street and the banks, thus sowing the seeds of class discontent. When economic trouble hits, free markets and free trade often are blamed, while the harmful effects of a fiat monetary system are ignored. We deceive ourselves that all is well with the economy, and ignore the fundamental flaws that are a source of growing discontent among those who have not shared in the abundance of recent years.

Few understand that our consumption and apparent wealth is dependent on a current account deficit of $800 billion per year. This deficit shows that much of our prosperity is based on borrowing rather than a true increase in production. Statistics show year after year that our productive manufacturing jobs continue to go overseas. This phenomenon is not seen as a consequence of the international fiat monetary system, where the United States government benefits as the issuer of the world's reserve currency.

Government officials consistently claim that inflation is in check at barely 2%, but middle class Americans know that their purchasing power--especially when it comes to housing, energy, medical care, and school tuition-- is shrinking much faster than 2% each year.

Even if prices were held in check, in spite of our monetary inflation, concentrating on CPI distracts from the real issue. We must address the important consequences of Fed manipulation of interest rates. When interests rates are artificially low, below market rates, insidious mal-investment and excessive indebtedness inevitably bring about the economic downturn that everyone dreads.

We look at GDP numbers to reassure ourselves that all

is well, yet a growing number of Americans still do not enjoy the higher standard of living that monetary inflation brings to the privileged few. Those few have access to the newly created money first, before its value is diluted.

For example: Before the breakdown of the Bretton Woods system, CEO income was about 30 times the average worker's pay. Today, it's closer to 500 times. It's hard to explain this simply by market forces and increases in productivity. One Wall Street firm last year gave out bonuses totaling $16.5 billion. There's little evidence that this represents free market capitalism.

In 2006 dollars, the minimum wage was $9.50 before the 1971 breakdown of Bretton Woods. Today that dollar is worth $5.15. Congress congratulates itself for raising the minimum wage by mandate, but in reality it has lowered the minimum wage by allowing the Fed to devalue the dollar. We must consider how the growing inequalities created by our monetary system will lead to social discord.

GDP purportedly is now growing at 3.5%, and everyone seems pleased. What we fail to understand is how much government entitlement spending contributes to the increase in the GDP. Rebuilding infrastructure destroyed by hurricanes, which simply gets us back to even, is considered part of GDP growth. Wall Street profits and salaries, pumped up by the Fed's increase in money, also contribute to GDP statistical growth. Just buying military weapons that contribute nothing to the well being of our citizens, sending money down a rat hole, contributes to GDP growth! Simple price increases caused by Fed monetary inflation contribute to nominal GDP growth. None of these factors represent any kind of real increases in economic output. So we should not carelessly cite misleading GDP figures which don't truly reflect what is happening in the economy. Bogus GDP figures explain in part why so many people are feeling squeezed despite our supposedly booming economy.

But since our fiat dollar system is not going away anytime soon, it would benefit Congress and the American
people to bring more transparency to how and why
Fed monetary policy functions.

For starters, the Federal Reserve should:

Begin publishing the M3 statistics again. Let us see the
numbers that most accurately reveal how much new
money the Fed is pumping into the world economy.

 Tell us exactly what the President's Working Group
on Financial Markets does and why.

Explain how interest rates are set. Conservatives pro-
fess to support free markets, without wage and price
controls. Yet the most important price of all, the price
of money as determined by interest rates, is set arbitrarily in secret by the Fed rather than by markets!
Why is this policy written in stone? Why is there no
congressional input at least?

Change legal tender laws to allow constitutional legal tender (commodity money) to compete domestically with the dollar.

How can a policy of steadily debasing our currency be defended morally, knowing what harm it causes to those who still believe in saving money and assuming responsibility for themselves in their retirement years? Is it any wonder we are a nation of debtors rather than savers?

We need more transparency in how the Federal Reserve carries out monetary policy, and we need it soon.

U.S. House. Committee on Financial Services.
Monetary Policy and the State of the Economy, Part I.
110th Cong., 1st sess., 15 February 2007. Washington, D.C.:
G.P.O., 2007.

What is Free Trade?

**A Speech by Ron Paul on May 2, 2000
on the floor of the US House of Representatives.**

Mr. PAUL. Madam Speaker, I asked for this Special Order this evening to talk about trade. We are going to be dealing with permanent normal trade relations with China here soon, and there is also a privileged resolution that will be brought to the floor that I have introduced, H.J.Res. 90. The discussion in the media and around the House floor has been rather clear about the permanent normal trade status, but there has not been a whole lot of talk yet about whether or not we should even really be in the World Trade Organization.

I took this time mainly because I think there is a lot of misunderstanding about what free trade is. There are not a whole lot of people who get up and say I am opposed to free trade, and many of those who say they are for free trade quite frankly I think they have a distorted definition of what free trade really is.

I would like to spend some time this evening talking a little bit about that, because as a strict constitutionalist and one who endorses laissez-faire capitalism, I do believe in free trade; and there are good reasons why countries should trade with each other.

The first reason I would like to mention is a moral reason. There is a moral element involved in trade, because when governments come in and regulate how citizens spend their money, they are telling them what they can do or cannot do. In a free society, individuals who earn money should be allowed to spend the money the way they want. So if they find that they prefer to buy a car from Japan rather than Detroit, they basically have the moral right to spend their money as they see fit and those kinds of choices should not be made by government. So there is a definite moral argument for free trade.

Patrick Henry many years ago touched on this when he said, `You are not to inquire how your trade may be increased nor how you are to become a great and powerful people but how your liberties may be secured, for liberty ought to be the direct end of your government.' We have not heard much talk of liberty with regards to trade, but we do hear a lot about enhancing one's ability to make more money overseas with trading with other nations. But the argument, the moral argument, itself should be enough to convince one in a free society that we should never hamper or interfere with free trade.

When the colonies did not thrive well prior to the Constitution, two of the main reasons why the Constitutional Convention was held was, one, there was no unified currency, that provided a great deal of difficulty in trading among the States, and also trade barriers are among the States.

Even our Constitution was designed to make sure that there were not trade barriers, and this was what the interstate commerce clause was all about. Unfortunately though, in this century the interstate commerce clause has been taken and twisted around and is the excuse for regulating even trade within a State. Not only interstate trade, but even activities within a State has nothing to do with interstate trade. They use the interstate commerce clause as an excuse, which is a wild distortion of the original intent of the Constitution, but free trade among the States having a unified currency and breaking down the barriers certainly was a great benefit for the development and the industrialization of the United States.

The second argument for free trade is an economic argument. There is a benefit to free trade. Free trade means that you will not have high tariffs and barriers so you cannot buy products and you cannot exert this freedom of choice by buying outside. If you have a restricted majority and you can evenly buy from within, it means you are protecting industries that may not be doing a very good job, and there is not enough competition.

It is conceded that probably it was a blessing in disguise when the automobile companies in this country were having trouble in the 1970s, because the American consumer was not buying the automobiles, the better automobiles were coming in, and it should not have been a surprise to anybody that all of a sudden the American cars got to be much better automobiles and they were able to compete.

There is a tremendous economic benefit to the competition by being able to buy overseas. The other economic argument is that in order to keep a product out, you put on a tariff, a protective tariff. A tariff is a tax. We should not confuse that, we should not think tariff is something softer than a tax in doing something good. A tariff is a tax on the consumer. So those American citizens who want to buy products at lower prices are forced to be taxed.

If you have poor people in this country trying to make it on their own and they are not on welfare, but they can buy clothes or shoes or an automobile or anything from overseas, they are tremendously penalized by forcing them to pay higher prices by buying domestically.

The competition is what really encourages producers to produce better products at lower costs and keep the prices down. If one believes in free trade, they do not enter into free trade for the benefit of somebody else. There is really no need for reciprocity. Free trade is beneficial because it is a moral right. Free trade is beneficial because there is an economic advantage to buying products at a certain price and the competition is beneficial.

There really are no costs in the long run. Free trade does not require management. It is implied here on conversation on the House floor so often that free trade is equivalent to say we will turn over the management of trade to the World Trade Organization, which serves special interests. Well, that is not free trade; that is a misunderstanding of free trade.

Free trade means you can buy and sell freely without interference. You do not need international management. Certainly, if we are not going to have our own government manage our own affairs, we do not want an international body to manage these international trades.

Another thing that free trade does not imply is that this opens up the doors to subsidies. Free trade does not mean subsidies, but inevitably as soon as we start trading with somebody, we accept the notion of managed trade by the World Trade Organization, but immediately we start giving subsidies to our competitors.

If our American companies and our American workers have to compete, the last thing they should ever be required to do is pay some of their tax money to the Government, to send subsidies to their competitors; and that is what is happening. They are forced to subsidize their competitors on foreign aid. They support their competitors overseas at the World Bank. They subsidize their competitors in the Export/Import Bank, the Overseas Private Investment Corporation.

We literally encourage the exportation of jobs by providing overseas protection in insurance that cannot be bought in the private sector. Here a company in the United States goes overseas for cheap labor, and if, for political or economic reasons, they go bust, who bails them out. It is the American taxpayer, once again, the people who are struggling and have to compete with the free trade.

It is so unfair to accept this notion that free trade is synonymous with permitting these subsidies overseas, and, essentially, that is what is happening all the time. Free trade should never mean that through the management of trade that it endorses the notion of retaliation and also to stop dumping.

This whole idea that all of a sudden if somebody comes in with a product with a low price that you can immediately get it stopped and retaliate, and this is all done in the name of free trade, it could be something one endorses. They might argue that they endorse this type of managed trade and subsidized trade; but what is wrong, and I want to make this clear, what is wrong is to call it free trade, because that is not free trade.

Most individuals that I know who promote free trade around Washington, D.C., do not really either understand what free trade is or they do not really endorse it. And they are very interested in the management aspect, because some of the larger companies have a much bigger clout with the World Trade Organization than would the small farmers, small rancher or small businessman because they do not have the same access to the World Trade Organization.

For instance, there has been a big fight in the World Trade Organization with bananas. The Europeans are fighting with the Americans over exportation of bananas. Well, bananas are not grown in Europe and they are not grown in the United States, and yet that is one of the big issues of managed trade, for the benefit of some owners of corporations that are overseas that make big donations to our political parties. That is not coincidental.

So powerful international financial individuals go to the World Trade Organization to try to get an edge on their competitor. If their competitor happens to be doing a better job and selling a little bit lower, then they come immediately to the World Trade Organization and say, Oh, you have to stop them. That is dumping. We certainly do not want to give the consumers the benefit of having a lower price.

So this to me is important, that we try to be clear on how we define free trade, and we should not do this by accepting the idea that management of trade, as well as subsidizing trade and calling it free trade is just not right. Free trade is the ability of an individual or a corporation to buy goods and spend their money as they see fit, and this provides tremendous economic benefits.

The third benefit of free trade, which has been known for many, many centuries, has been the peace effect from trade. It is known that countries that trade with each other and depend on each other for certain products and where the trade has been free and open and communications are free and open and travel is free and open, they are very less likely to fight wars. I happen to personally think this is one of the greatest benefits of free trade, that it leads us to policies that direct us away from military confrontation.

Managed trade and subsidized trade do not qualify. I will mention just a little later why I think it does exactly the opposite.

There is a little bit more to the trade issue than just the benefits of free trade, true free trade, and the disadvantages of managed trade, because we are dealing now when we have a vote on the normal trade status with China, as well as getting out of the World Trade Organization, we are dealing with the issue of sovereignty. The Constitution is very clear. Article I, section 8, gives the Congress the responsibility of dealing with international trade. It does not delegate it to the President, it does not delegate it to a judge, it does not delegate it to an international management organization like the World Trade Organization.

International trade management is to be and trade law is to be dealt with by the U.S. Congress, and yet too often the Congress has been quite willing to renege on that responsibility through fast-track legislation and deliver this authority to our President, as well as delivering through agreements, laws being passed and treaties, delivering this authority to international bodies such as the UN-IMF-World Trade Organizations, where they make decisions that affect us and our national sovereignty.

The World Trade Organization has been in existence for 5 years. We voted to join the World Trade Organization in the fall of 1994 in the lame duck session after the Republicans took over the control of the House and Senate, but before the new Members were sworn in. So a lame duck session was brought up and they voted, and by majority vote we joined the World Trade Organization, which, under the Constitution, clearly to anybody who has studied the Constitution, is a treaty. So we have actually even invoked a treaty by majority vote.

This is a serious blunder, in my estimation, the way we have dealt with this issue, and we have accepted the idea that we will remain a member based on this particular vote.

Fortunately, in 1994 there was a provision put in the bill that said that any member could bring up a privileged resolution that gives us a chance at least to say is this a good idea to be in the World Trade Organization, or is it not? Now, my guess is that we do not have the majority of the U.S. Congress that thinks it is a bad idea. But I am wondering about the majority of the American people, and I am wondering about the number of groups now that are growing wary of the membership in the World Trade Organization, when you look at what happened in Seattle, as well as demonstrations here in D.C. So there is a growing number of people from various aspects of the political spectrum who are now saying, what does this membership mean to us? Is it good or is it bad? A lot of them are coming down on the side of saying it is bad.

Now, it is also true that some who object to membership in the World Trade Organization happen to be conservative free enterprisers, and others who object are coming from the politics of the left. But there is agreement on both sides of this issue dealing with this aspect, and it has to do with the sovereignty issue.

There may be some labor law and there may be some environmental law that I would object to, but I more strenuously object to the World Trade Organization dictating to us what our labor law ought to be and what our environmental law ought to be. I highly resent the notion that the World Trade Organization can dictate to us tax law.

We are currently under review and the World Trade Organization has ruled against the United States because we have given a tax break to our overseas company, and they have ruled against us and said that this tax break is a tax subsidy, language which annoys me to no end. They have given us until October 1 to get rid of that tax break for our corporations, so they are telling us, the U.S. Congress, what we have to do with tax law.

You say, oh, that cannot be. We do not have to do what they tell us. Well, technically we do not have to, but we will not be a very good member, and this is what we agreed to in the illegal agreement. Certainly it was not a legitimate treaty that we signed. But in this agreement we have come up and said that we would obey what the WTO says.

Our agreement says very clearly that any ruling by the WTO, the Congress is obligated to change the law. This is the interpretation and this is what we signed. This is a serious challenge, and we should not accept so easily this idea that we will just go one step further.

This has not just happened 5 years ago, there has been a gradual erosion of the concept of national sovereignty. It occurred certainly after World War II with the introduction of the United Nations, and now, under current conditions, we do not even ask the

Congress to declare war, yet we still fight a lot of wars. We send troops all over the world and we are involved in combat all the time, and our Presidents tell us they get the authority from a UN resolution. So we have gradually lost the concept of national sovereignty.

I want to use a quote from somebody that I consider rather typical of the establishment. We talk about the establishment, but nobody ever knows exactly who they are. But I will name this individual who I think is pretty typical of the establishment, and that is Walter Cronkite. He says, `We need not only an executive to make international law, but we need the military forces to enforce that law and the judicial system to bring the criminals to justice in an international government.'

`But,' he goes on to say, and this he makes very clear, and this is what we should be aware of, `the American people are going to begin to realize that perhaps they are going to have to yield some sovereignty to an international body to enforce world law, and I think that is going to come to other people as well.'

So it is not like it has been hidden, it is not like it is a secret. It is something that those who disagree with me about liberty and the Constitution, they believe in internationalism and the World Trade Organization and the United Nations, and they certainly have the right to that belief, but it contradicts everything America stands for and it contradicts our Constitution, so, therefore, we should not allow this to go unchallenged.

Now, the whole idea that treaties could be passed and undermine the ability of our Congress to pass legislation or undermine our Constitution, this was thought about and talked about by the founders of this country. They were rather clear on the idea that a treaty, although the treaty can become the law of the land, a treaty could never be an acceptable law of the land if it amended or changed the Constitution. That would be ridiculous, and they made that very clear.

It could have the effect of the law of the land, as long as it was a legitimate constitutional agreement that we entered into. But Thomas Jefferson said if the treaty power is unlimited, then we do not have a Constitution. Surely the President and the Senate cannot do by treaty what the whole government is interdicted from doing in any way.

So that is very important. We cannot just sit back and accept the idea that the World Trade Organization, we have entered into it, it was not a treaty, it was an agreement, but we have entered into it, and the agreement says we have to do what they tell us, even if it contradicts the whole notion that it is the Congress' and people's responsibility to pass their own laws with regard to the environment, with regard to labor and with regard to tax law.

So I think this is important material. I think this is an important subject, a lot more important than just the vote to trade with China. I think we should trade with

China. I think we should trade with Cuba. I think we should trade with everybody possible, unless we are at war with them. I do not think we should have sanctions against Iran, Iraq or Libya, and it does not make much sense to me to be struggling and fighting and giving more foreign aid to a country like China, and at the same time we have sanctions on and refuse to trade and talk with Cuba. That does not make a whole lot of sense. Yet those who believe and promote trade with China are the ones who will be strongly objecting to trade with Cuba and these other countries. So I think a little bit more consistency on this might be better for all of us.

Alexander Hamilton also talked about this. He said a treaty cannot be made which alters the Constitution of the country or which infringes any expressed exception to the powers of the Constitution of the United States.

So these were the founders talking about this, and yet

we have drifted a long way. It does not happen overnight. It has been over a 50-year period. Five years ago we went one step further. First we accepted the idea that international finance would be regulated by the IMF. Then we accepted the idea that the World Bank, which was supposed to help the poor people of the world and redistribute wealth, they have redistributed a lot of wealth, but most of it ended up in the hands of wealthy individuals and wealthy politicians. But the poor people of the world never get helped by these programs. Now, 5 years ago we have accepted the notion that the World Trade Organization will bring about order in trade around the country.

Well, since that time we have had a peso crisis in Mexico and we had a crisis with currencies in Southeast Asia. So I would say that the management of finances with the IMF as well as the World Trade Organization has been very unsuccessful, and even if one does not accept my constitutional argument that we should not be doing this, we should at least consider the fact that what we are doing is not very successful.

Cong. Rec. 2 May 2000: H2393-H2398

<u>Protection of Individuals over Societies</u>

Despite the recent national hysteria over the threat of terrorist attacks our society continues moving towards the emphasis of the quality of individuals and their thoughts over the quality of societal stability and group safety. As Ben Franklin argued at the founding of our nation, we must not sacrifice liberty for security, or else we will end up with neither.

Since 9/11 we have not had another terrorist attack on our soil. This should not be surprising because in one swoop Bin Laden managed to set in motion a 7 year long process where we have destroyed ourselves and everything we believe in. George W. Bush has been the greatest President Al Qaeda could have hoped for, and he has restricted American freedoms to an extent that may not be undone without the kind of drastic correction that a Ron Paul presidency could implement.

Fear is a favorite weapon of George W. Bush and his administration. He has terrified the press and the American people into silence regarding his failure and incompetence. Secrecy is not a tool of the strong, it is the refuge of the weak. Secrecy is the moral and intellectual equivalent of hiding under the bedclothes. But the fear of the so-called "security moms" and others granted Bush a blank check to attack anyone who opposed him.

McCarthyism is rampant at the moment, though it is less noticed. Those who oppose the President are coddling terrorists, and they don't support the troops. The press doesn't have the courage it did in the 1950's to stand up to George Bush and his illegal detainments and his trials of civilians in military courts. The government is trying to provide for the safety of individuals, and as usual is inconveniencing millions and outright attacking thousands without improving real security whatsoever. The targets of the government are different than were the targets of McCarthy's committee. Middle class America does not feel threatened, and thus they are largely uninterested in the plight of those imprisoned and sent overseas to be tortured. Nor does the press feel that reporting these events will sell, so they are not mentioned.

A free society is a double edged sword: we trade in the security of facism for the freedom to express ourselves and to act without fear of government retaliation. Governments have always proved inadequate when they attempt to regulate the lives of individuals, and the Bush Administration is perhaps the best example of this failure in history.

Big Government Solutions Don't Work

The Law of Opposites

A speech by Ron Paul in the US House of

Representatives on September 7, 2006.

Politicians throughout history have tried to solve every problem conceivable to man, always failing to recognize that many of the problems we face result from previous so-called political solutions. Government cannot be the answer to every human ill. Continuing to view more government as the solution to problems will only make matters worse.

Not too long ago, I spoke on this floor about why I believe Americans are so angry in spite of rosy government economic reports. The majority of Americans are angry, disgusted, and frustrated that so little is being done in Congress to solve their problems. The fact is a majority of American citizens expect the federal government to provide for every need, without considering whether government causes many economic problems in the first place. This certainly is an incentive for politicians to embrace the role of omnipotent problem solvers, since nobody asks first whether they, the politicians themselves, are at fault.

At home I'm frequently asked about my frustration with Congress, since so many reform proposals go unheeded. I jokingly reply, "No, I'm never frustrated, because I have such low expectations." But the American people have higher expectations, and without forthcoming solutions, are beyond frustrated with their government.

If solutions to America's problems won't be found in the frequent clamor for more government, it's still up

to Congress to explain how our problems develop--
and how solutions can be found in an atmosphere of
liberty, private property, and a free market order. It's
up to us to demand radical change from our failed policy of foreign military interventionism. Robotic
responses to the clichés of big government intervention in our lives are unbecoming to members who
were elected to offer ideas and solutions. We must
challenge the status quo of our economic and political
system.

Many things have contributed to the mess we're in.
Bureaucratic management can never compete with the
free market in solving problems. Central economic
planning doesn't work. Just look at the failed systems
of the 20th century. Welfarism is an example of central economic planning. Paper money, money created
out of thin air to accommodate welfarism and government deficits, is not only silly, it's unconstitutional.
No matter how hard the big spenders try to convince
us otherwise, deficits do matter. But lowering the

deficit through higher taxes won't solve anything.

Nothing will change in Washington until it's recognized that the ultimate driving force behind most politicians is obtaining and holding power. And money from special interests drives the political process. Money and power are important only because the government wields power not granted by the Constitution. A limited, constitutional government would not tempt special interests to buy the politicians who wield power. The whole process feeds on itself. Everyone is rewarded by ignoring constitutional restraints, while expanding and complicating the entire bureaucratic state.

Even when it's recognized that we're traveling down the wrong path, the lack of political courage and the desire for reelection results in ongoing support for the pork-barrel system that serves special interests. A safe middle ground, a don't-rock-the-boat attitude, too often is rewarded in Washington, while meaningful solutions tend to offend those who are in charge of the gigantic PAC/lobbyist empire that calls the shots in Washington. Most members are rewarded by reelection for accommodating and knowing how to work the system.

Though there's little difference between the two parties, the partisan fights are real. Instead of debates about philosophy, the partisan battles are about who will wield the gavels. True policy debates are rare; power struggles are real and ruthless. And yet we all know that power corrupts.

Both parties agree on monetary, fiscal, foreign and entitlement policies. Unfortunately, neither party has much concern for civil liberties. Both parties are split over trade, with mixed debates between outright protectionists and those who endorse government-managed trade agreements that masquerade as "free trade." It's virtually impossible to find anyone who supports hands-off free trade, defended by the moral right of all citizens to spend their money as they see fit, without being subject any special interest.

The big government nanny-state is based on the assumption that free markets can't provide the maximum good for the largest number of people. It assumes people are not smart or responsible enough to take care of themselves, and thus their needs must be filled through the government's forcible redistribution of wealth. Our system of intervention assumes that politicians and bureaucrats have superior knowledge, and are endowed with certain talents that produce efficiency. These assumptions don't seem to hold much water, of course, when we look at agencies like FEMA. Still, we expect the government to manage monetary and economic policy, the medical system, and the educational system, and then wonder why we have problems with the cost and efficiency of all these programs.

On top of this, the daily operation of Congress reflects

the power of special interests, not the will of the people- regardless of which party is in power.

Critically important legislation comes up for votes late in the evening, leaving members little chance to read or study the bills. Key changes are buried in conference reports, often containing new legislation not even mentioned in either the House or Senate versions.

Conferences were meant to compromise two different positions in the House and Senate bills-- not to slip in new material that had not been mentioned in either bill.

Congress spends hundreds of billions of dollars in "emergency" supplemental bills to avoid the budgetary rules meant to hold down the deficit. Wartime spending money is appropriated and attached to emergency relief funds, making it difficult for politicians to resist.

The principle of the pork barrel is alive and well, and it shows how huge appropriations are passed easily with supporters of the system getting their share for their district.

Huge omnibus spending bills, introduced at the end of the legislative year, are passed without scrutiny. No one individual knows exactly what is in the bill.

In the process, legitimate needs and constitutional responsibilities are frequently ignored. Respect for private property rights is ignored. Confidence in the free market is lost or misunderstood. Our tradition of self-reliance is mocked as archaic.

Lack of real choice in economic and personal decisions is commonplace. It seems that too often the only choice we're given is between prohibitions or subsidies. Never is it said, "Let the people decide on things like stem cell research or alternative medical treatments."

Nearly everyone endorses exorbitant taxation; the only debate is about who should pay—either tax the producers and the rich or tax the workers and the poor through inflation and outsourcing jobs.

Both politicians and the media place blame on everything except bad policy authored by Congress. Scapegoats are needed, since there's so much blame to go around and so little understanding as to why we're in such a mess.

In 1920s and 1930s Europe, as the financial system collapsed and inflation raged, it was commonplace to blame the Jews. Today in America the blame is spread out: Illegal immigrants, Muslims, big business (whether they get special deals from the government or not), price gouging oil companies (regardless of the circumstances), and labor unions. Ignorance of economics and denial of the political power system that prevails in D.C. make it possible for Congress to shift blame.

Since we're not on the verge of mending our ways, the problems will worsen and the blame games will get much more vicious. Shortchanging a large segment of our society surely will breed conflict that could get out of control. This is a good reason for us to cast aside politics as usual and start finding some reliable answers to our problems.

Politics as usual is aided by the complicity of the media. Economic ignorance, bleeding heart emotionalism, and populist passion pervade our major networks and cable channels. This is especially noticeable when the establishment seeks to unify the people behind an illegal, unwise war. The propaganda is well-coordinated   by   the media/government/military/industrial complex. This collusion is worse than when state- owned media do the same thing. In countries where everyone knows the media produces government propaganda, people remain wary of what they hear. In the United States the media are considered free and independent, thus the propaganda is accepted with less questioning.

One of the major reasons we've drifted from the Founders vision of liberty in the Constitution was the division of the concept of freedom into two parts. Instead of freedom being applied equally to social and economic transactions, it has come to be thought of as two different concepts. Some in Congress now protect economic liberty and market choices, but ignore personal liberty and private choices. Others defend personal liberty, but concede the realm of property and economic transactions to government control.

There should be no distinction between commercial speech and political speech. With no consistent moral defense of true liberty, the continued erosion of personal and property rights is inevitable. This careless disregard for liberty, our traditions, and the Constitution have brought us disaster, with a foreign policy of military interventionism supported by the leadership of both parties. Hopefully, some day this will be radically changed.

The Law of Opposites

Everyone is aware of the Law of Unintended Consequences. Most members of Congress understand that government actions can have unintended consequences, yet few quit voting for government "solutions" -- always hoping there won't be any particular unintended consequences this time. They keep hoping there will be less harmful complications from the "solution" that they currently support. Free market economics teaches that for every government action to solve an economic problem, two new ones are created. The same unwanted results occur with foreign policy meddling.

The Law of Opposites is just a variation of the Law of Unintended Consequences. When we attempt to achieve a certain goal-- like, "make the world safe for democracy," a grandiose scheme of World War I-- one can be sure the world will become less safe and less democratic regardless of the motivation.

The 1st World War was sold to the American people as the war to end all wars. Instead, history shows it was the war that caused the 20th century to be the most war-torn century in history. Our entry into World War I helped lead us into World War II, the Cold War, the Korean War, and the Vietnam War. Even our current crisis in the Middle East can be traced to the great wars of the 20th century. Though tens of millions of deaths are associated with these wars, we haven't learned a thing.

We went into Korea by direction of the United Nations, not a congressional declaration of war, to unify Korea. And yet that war ensured that Korea remains divided to this day; our troops are still there. South Korea today is much more willing to reconcile differences with North Korea, and yet we obstruct such efforts. It doesn't make much sense.

We went into Vietnam and involved ourselves unnecessarily in a civil war to bring peace and harmony to that country. We lost 60,000 troops and spent hundreds of billions of dollars, yet failed to achieve victory. Ironically, since losing in Vietnam we now have a better relationship with them than ever. We now trade, invest, travel, and communicate with a unified, western-leaning country that is catching on rather quickly to capitalist ways. This policy, not military confrontation, is exactly what the Constitution permits and the Founders encouraged in our relationship with others.

This policy should apply to both friends and perceived enemies. Diplomacy and trade can accomplish goals that military intervention cannot-- and they certainly are less costly.

In both instances--Korea and Vietnam-- neither country attacked us, and neither country posed a threat to our security. In neither case did we declare war. All of the fighting and killing was based on lies, miscalculations, and the failure to abide by constitutional restraint with regards to war.

When goals are couched in terms of humanitarianism, sincere or not, the results are inevitably bad. Foreign interventionism requires the use of force. First, the funds needed to pursue a particular policy require that taxes be forcibly imposed on the American people, either directly or indirectly through inflation. Picking sides in foreign countries only increases the chances of antagonism toward us. Too often foreign economic and military support means impoverishing the poor in America and enhancing the rich ruling classes in poor countries. When sanctions are used against one undesirable regime, it squelches resistance to the very regimes we're trying to undermine. Forty years of sanctions against Castro have left him in power, and fomented continued hatred and blame from the Cuban people directed at us. Trade with Cuba likely would have accomplished the opposite, as it has in Vietnam,

China, and even in the Eastern Block nations of the old Soviet empire.

We spend billions of dollars in Afghanistan and Colombia to curtail drug production. No evidence exists that it helps. In fact, drug production and corruption have increased. We close our eyes to it because the reasons we're in Colombia and Afghanistan are denied.

Obviously, we are not putting forth the full effort required to capture Osama bin Laden. Instead, our occupation of Afghanistan further inflames the Muslim radicals that came of age with their fierce resistance to the Soviet occupation of a Muslim country. Our occupation merely serves as a recruiting device for al Qaeda, which has promised retaliation for our presence in their country. We learned nothing after first allying ourselves with Osama bin Laden when he applied this same logic toward the Soviets. The net result of our invasion and occupation of Afghanistan has been to miss capturing bin Laden, assist al Qaeda's recruitment, stimulate more drug production, lose hundreds of American lives, and allow spending billions of American taxpayer dollars with no end in sight.

Bankruptcy seems to be the only way we will reconsider the foolishness of this type of occupation. It's time for us to wake up.

Our policy toward Iran for the past 50 years is every bit as disconcerting. It makes no sense unless one concedes that our government is manipulated by those who seek physical control over the vast oil riches of the Middle East and egged on by Israel's desires.

We have attacked the sovereignty of Iran on two occasions, and are in the process of threatening her for the third time. In 1953, the U.S. and British overthrew the democratically elected Mohammad Mossadegh and installed the Shah. His brutal regime lasted over 25 years, and ended with the Ayatollah taking power in 1979. Our support for the Shah incited the radicalization of the Shiite Clerics in Iran, resulting in the hostage takeover.

In the 1980s we provided weapons-- including poisonous gas-- to Saddam Hussein as we supported his invasion of Iran. These events are not forgotten by the Iranians, who see us once again looking for another confrontation with them. We insist that the UN ignore the guarantees under the NPT that grant countries like Iran the right to enrich uranium. The pressure on the UN and the threats we cast toward Iran are quite harmful to the cause of peace. They are entirely unnecessary and serve no useful purpose. Our policy toward Iran is much more likely to result in her getting a nuclear weapon than prevent it.

Our own effort at democratizing Iran has resulted instead in radicalizing a population whose instincts are to like Americans and our economic system. Our meddling these past 50 years has only served to alien-ate and unify the entire country against us.

Though our officials only see Iran as an enemy, as does Israel, our policies in the Middle East these past 5 years have done wonders to strengthen Iran's political and military position in the region. We have totally ignored serious overtures by the Iranians to negotiate with us before hostilities broke out in Iraq in 2003. Both immediately after 9/11, and especially at the time of our invasion of Iraq in 2003, Iran, partially out of fear and realism, honestly sought reconciliation and offered to help the U.S. in its battle against al Qaeda. They were rebuked outright. Now Iran is negotiating from a much stronger position, principally as a result of our overall Middle East policy.

We accommodated Iran by severely weakening the Taliban in Afghanistan on Iran's eastern borders. On Iran's western borders we helped the Iranians by elim-inating their arch enemy, Saddam Hussein. Our invasion in Iraq and the resulting chaos have inadvertently delivered up a large portion of Iraq to the Iranians, as the majority Shiites in Iraq ally themselves with Iranians.

The U.S./Israeli plan to hit Hezbollah in Lebanon before taking on Iran militarily has totally backfired. Now Hezbollah, an ally of Iran, has been made stronger than ever with the military failure to rout Hezbollah from southern Lebanon. Before the U.S./Israeli invasion of Lebanon, Hezbollah was supported by 20% of the population, now it's revered by 80%. A democratic election in Lebanon cannot now serve the interest of the U.S. or Israel. It would only support the cause of radical clerics in Iran.

Demanding an election in Palestinian Gaza resulted in enhancing the power of Hamas. The U.S. and Israel promptly rejected the results. So much for our support for democratically elected government.

Our support for dictatorial Arab leaders is a thorn in the side of the large Muslim population in the Middle East, and one of the main reasons Osama bin Laden declared war against us. We talk of democracy and self-determination, but the masses of people in the Middle East see through our hypocrisy when we support the Sunni secular dictators in Saudi Arabia, Egypt, and Jordan and at one time, Saddam Hussein.

In the late 1970s and the 1980s the CIA spent over $4 billion on a program called "Operation Cyclone." This was our contribution to setting up training schools in Pakistan and elsewhere, including the U.S. itself, to teach "sabotage skills." The purpose was to use these individuals in fighting our enemies in the Middle East, including the Soviets. But as one could predict, this effort has come back to haunt us, as our radical ally Osama bin Laden turned his fury against us after routing the Soviets. It is estimated that over 12,000 fighters were trained in the camps we set up in Afghanistan. They were taught how to make bombs, carry out sabotage, and use guerrilla war tactics. And now we're on the receiving end of this U.S. financed program-- hardly a good investment.

It's difficult to understand why our policy makers aren't more cautious in their efforts to police the world, once it's realized how unsuccessful we have been. It seems they always hope that next time our efforts won't come flying back in our face.

Our failed efforts in Iraq continue to drain our resources, costing us dearly both in lives lost and dollars spent. And there's no end in sight. No consideration is given for rejecting our obsession with a worldwide military presence, which rarely if ever directly enhances our security. A much stronger case can be made that our policy of protecting our worldwide interests actually does the opposite by making us weaker, alienating our allies, inciting more hatred, and provoking our enemies. The more we have interfered in the Middle East in the last 50 years, the greater the danger has become for an attack on us. The notion that Arab/Muslim radicals are motivated to attack us because of our freedoms and prosperity, and not our unwelcome presence in their countries, is dangerous and silly.

We were told we needed to go into Iraq because our old ally, Saddam Hussein, had weapons of mass destruction-- yet no weapons of mass destruction were found.

We were told we needed to occupy Iraq to remove al Qaeda, yet al Qaeda was nowhere to be found and now it's admitted it had nothing to do with 9/11. Yet today, Iraq is infested with al Qaeda-- achieving exactly the opposite of what we sought to do.

We were told that we needed to secure "our oil" to protect our economy and to pay for our invasion and occupation. Instead, the opposite has resulted: Oil production is down, oil prices are up, and no oil profits have been used to pay the bills.

We were told that a regime change in Iraq would help us in our long-time fight with Iran, yet everything we have done in Iraq has served the interests of Iran.

We're being told in a threatening and intimidating fashion that, "If America were to pull out before Iraq could defend itself, the consequences would be absolutely predictable and absolutely disastrous." I'm convinced that the Law of Opposites could well apply here. Going into Iraq we know produced exactly the opposite results of what was predicted: Leaving also likely will have results opposite of those we're being frightened with. Certainly leaving Vietnam at the height of the Cold War did not result in the disaster predicted by the advocates of the Domino Theory-- an inevitable Communist takeover of the entire Far East.

We're constantly being told that we cannot abandon Iraq and we are obligated to stay forever if necessary. This admonition is similar to a rallying cry from a determined religious missionary bent on proselytizing to the world with a particular religious message. Conceding that leaving may not be a panacea for Iraqi tranquility, this assumption ignores two things. One, our preemptive war ignited the Iraqi civil war, and two, abandoning the Iraqi people is not the question. The real question is whether or not we should abandon the American people by forcing them to pay for an undeclared war with huge economic and human costs, while placing our national security in greater jeopardy by ignoring our borders and serious problems here at home.

In our attempt to make Iraq a better place, we did great harm to Iraqi Christians. Before our invasion in 2003 there were approximately 1.2 million living in Iraq. Since then over half have been forced to leave due to persecution and violence. Many escaped to Syria. With the neo-cons wanting to attack Syria, how long will they be safe there? The answer to the question, "Aren't we better off without Saddam Hussein," is not an automatic yes for Iraqi Christians.

We've been told for decades that our policy of militarism and preemption in the Middle East is designed to provide security for Israel. Yet a very strong case can be made that Israel is more vulnerable than ever, with moderate Muslims being challenged by a growing majority of Islamic radicals. As the invincibility of the American and Israeli military becomes common knowledge, Israel's security is diminished and world opinion turns against her, especially after the failed efforts to remove the Hezbollah threat.

We were told that attacking and eliminating Hezbollah was required to diminish the Iranian threat against Israel. The results again were the opposite. This failed effort has only emboldened Iran.

The lack of success of conventional warfare-- the U.S. in Vietnam, the Soviets in Afghanistan, the U.S. in Iraq and Afghanistan, Israel in Lebanon-- should awaken our policy makers to our failure in war and diplomacy.

Yet all we propose are bigger bombs and more military force for occupation, rather than working to understand an entirely new generation of modern warfare.

Many reasons are given for our preemptive wars and military approach for spreading the American message of freedom and prosperity, which is an obvious impossibility. Our vital interests are always cited for justification, and it's inferred that those who do not support our militancy are unpatriotic. Yet the opposite is actually the case: Wise resistance to one's own government doing bad things requires a love of country, devotion to idealism, and respect for the Rule of Law.

In attempting to build an artificial and unwelcome Iraqi military, the harder we try, the more money we spend, and the more lives we lose, the stronger the real armies of Iraq become: the Sunni insurgency, the Bardr Brigade, the Sardr Mahdi Army, and the Kurdish militia.

The Kurds have already taken a bold step in this direction by hoisting a Kurdish flag and removing the Iraqi flag-- a virtual declaration of independence. Natural local forces are winning out over outside political forces.

We're looking in all the wrong places for an Iraqi army to bring stability to that country. The people have spoken and these troops that represent large segments of the population need no training. It's not a lack of training, weapons, or money that hinders our efforts to create a new superior Iraqi military. It's the lack of inspiration and support for such an endeavor that is missing. Developing borders and separating the various factions, which our policy explicitly prohibits, is the basic flaw in our plan for a forced, unified, western-style democracy for Iraq. Allowing self-determination for different regions is the only way to erase the artificial nature of Iraq-- an Iraq designed by western outsiders nearly 80 years ago. It's our obsession with control of the oil in the region, and imposing our will on the Middle East, and accommodating the demands of Israel that is the problem. And the American people are finally getting sick and tired of their sacrifices. It's time to stop the bleeding.

Instead we continue to hear the constant agitation for us to confront the Iranians with military action. Reasons to attack Iran make no more sense than our foolish preemptive war against Iraq. Fictitious charges and imaginary dangers are used to frighten the American people into accepting an attack on Iran. First it may only be sanctions, but later it will be bombs and possible ground troops if the neo-cons have their way. Many of the chicken-hawk neo-conservative advisors to the administration are highly critical of our current policy because it's not aggressive enough. They want more troops in Iraq, they want to attack Syria and Iran, and escalate the conflict in Lebanon.

We have a troop shortage, morale is low, and our military equipment is in bad shape, yet the neo-cons would not hesitate to spend, borrow, inflate, and reinstate the draft to continue their grandiose schemes in remaking the entire Middle East. Obviously a victory of this sort is not available, no matter what effort is made or how much money is spent.

Logic would tell us there's no way we will contemplate taking on Iran at this time. But logic did not prevail with our Iraq policy, and look at the mess we have there. Besides, both sides, the neo-con extremists and the radical Islamists, are driven by religious fervor. Both are convinced that God is on their side-- a strange assumption since theologically it's the same God.

Both sides of the war in the Middle East are driven by religious beliefs of omnipotence. Both sides endorse an eschatological theory regarding the forthcoming end of time. Both anticipate the return of God personified and as promised to each. Both sides are driven by a conviction of perfect knowledge regarding the Creator, and though we supposedly worship the same

God, each sees the other side as completely wrong and blasphemous. The religiously driven Middle East war condemns tolerance of the other's view. Advocates of restraint and the use of diplomacy are ridiculed as appeasers, and equivalent to supporting Nazism and considered un-American and un-Christian.

I find it amazing that we in this country seem determined to completely separate religious expression and the state, even to the detriment of the 1st Amendment. Yet we can say little about how Christian and Jewish religious beliefs greatly influences our policies in the Middle East. It should be the other way around. Religious expression, according to the 1st Amendment, cannot be regulated anywhere by Congress or the federal courts. But deeply held theological beliefs should never dictate our foreign policy. Being falsely accused of anti-Semitism and being a supporter of radical fascism is not an enviable position for any politician. Most realize it's best to be quiet and support our Middle East involvement.

Believing we have perfect knowledge of God's will, and believing government can manage our lives and world affairs, have caused a great deal of problems for man over the ages. When these two elements are combined they become especially dangerous. Liberty, by contrast, removes power from government and allows total freedom of choice in pursuing one's religious beliefs. The only solution to controlling political violence is to prohibit the use of force to pursue religious goals and reject government authority to mold the behavior of individuals.

Both are enamored with the so-called benefit that chaos offers to those promoting revolutionary changes. Both sides in situations like this always underestimate the determination of the opposition, and ignore the law of unintended consequences. They never consider that these policies might backfire.

Declaring war against Islamic fascism or terrorism is

vague and meaningless. This enemy we're fighting at the expense of our own liberties is purposely indefinable. Therefore the government will exercise wartime powers indefinitely. We've been fully warned to expect a long, long war.

The Islamic fascists are almost impossible to identify and cannot be targeted by our conventional weapons. Those who threaten us essentially are unarmed and stateless. Comparing them to Nazi Germany, a huge military power, is ridiculous. Labeling them as a unified force is a mistake. It's critical that we figure out why a growing number of Muslims are radicalized to the point of committing suicide terrorism against us. Our presence in their countries represents a failed policy that makes us less safe, not more.

These guerrilla warriors do not threaten us with tanks, gunboats, fighter planes, missiles, or nuclear weapons, nor do they have a history of aggression against the United States. Our enemy's credibility depends instead on the popular goal of ending our occupation of their country.

We must not forget that the 9/11 terrorists came principally from Saudi Arabia, not Iraq, Iran, Lebanon, or Syria. Iran has never in modern times invaded her neighbors, yet we worry obsessively that she may develop a nuclear weapon someday. Never mind that a radicalized Pakistan has nuclear weapons; our friend Musharraf won't lift a finger against Bin Laden, who most likely is hiding there. Our only defense against this emerging nuclear threat has been to use, and threaten to use, weapons that do not meet the needs of this new and different enemy.

Since resistance against the Iraq war is building here at home, hopefully it won't be too long before we abandon our grandiose scheme to rule the entire Middle East through intimidation and military confrontation.

Economic law eventually will prevail. Runaway military and entitlement spending cannot be sustained. We can tax the private economy only so much, and borrowing from foreigners is limited by the total foreign debt and our current account deficit. It will be difficult to continue this spending spree without significantly higher interest rates and further devaluation of the dollar. This all spells more trouble for our economy and certainly higher inflation. Our industrial base is shattered and our borders remain open to those who exploit our reeling entitlement system.

Economic realities will prevail, regardless of the enthusiasm by most members of Congress for a continued expansion of the welfare state and support for our dangerously aggressive foreign policy. The welfare/warfare state will come to an end when the dollar fails and the money simply runs out.

The overriding goal should then be to rescue our constitutional liberties, which have been steadily eroded by those who claim that sacrificing civil liberties is required and legitimate in times of war-- even the undeclared and vague war we're currently fighting.

A real solution to our problems will require a better understanding of, and greater dedication to, free markets and private property rights. It can't be done without restoring a sound, asset-backed currency. If we hope to restore any measure of constitutional government, we must abandon the policy of policing the world and keeping troops in every corner of the earth. Our liberties and our prosperity depend on it.

Cong. Rec. 7 September, 2006: H6357-H6361

The Wasted Opportunities
of the Bush Administration

George W. Bush took the greatest moment of national unity in 50 years, and wasted it pushing a narrow, opportunistic agenda which has created short term gains for his cronies and long term peril for our nation. The extent of his incompetence is visible for all to see. He has increased domestic and military spending and simultaneously cut taxes, expanding our national debt to nearly insurmountable levels. He has pushed faith based initiatives designed to promote Fundamentalist Christianity at the expense of all others. He has taken us to war without asking for sacrifice from anyone in the nation besides the mostly lower and middle class families who have members in the military. He has pushed the greatest military on earth to the breaking point, costing us the ability to respond to threats around the world and the ability to support and defend our homeland in time of need.

Secrecy is the refuge of the weak and incompetent. No nation hides its success. Secrecy allows fools to pretend they have thought about issues. Secrecy allows public arrogance to be coupled with utter failure.

From the outing of Valerie Plame and the Scooter Libby pardon we learned that the administration views secrecy and national security as tools to protect themselves and attack their enemies. They are purely selfish in their application of it. They will hide behind national security to keep from having to admit their failures, and then they will blatantly commit treason to reveal the covert identity of one of their enemies.

The End of Freedom

We are one bullet away from Fascism. Never since the great depression or perhaps even since the Civil War has the overthrow of the United States Government been so real a possibility. A hostile regime such as Iran or North Korea could destroy all of the freedoms Americans fought and died for if they managed to assassinate George W. Bush before he leaves office. Dick Cheney would almost certainly establish permanent martial law, and a new American dictatorship would be born. The Patriot Act granted the President the authority to suspend the constitution in event of "National Emergency." There would be no 2008 Presidential election, there would be no constitution. The only recourse would be a massive populist uprising to restore our government.

The Iraq war has seen massive growth of companies referred to as private security contractors. In previous wars organizations of this type were referred to as mercenary groups. These groups are staffed mainly by former US Military Personnel and are largely unregulated. Without exception they are lead by extraordinarily fanatical conservatives, and they have demonstrated time and again their disdain for human life. In previous wars, atrocities could sometimes be kept quiet, but the Iraq war is very different, and there are multiple YouTube videos in existence showing Blackwater personnel indiscriminately killing civilians and reveling in the doing of it. BlackWater's private army is headquartered less than 400 miles south of Washington DC. The temptation this presents to a panicked right wing President may very well be too much to resist.

But short of this nightmarish scenario, we have already seen the beginnings of a police state. It is a slippery slope to begin removing certain freedoms in the name of security. How many American citizens have been imprisoned simply because their name was similar to a terrorist? How many fear to speak because they know that any government attention will be negative? How many have lost their jobs and livelihood because they look like a "terrorist" ?

In the Name of Patriotism

(Who are the Patriots?)

A speech by Ron Paul in the US House of

Representatives on May 22, 2007

For some, patriotism is "the last refuge of a scoundrel." For others, it means dissent against a government's abuse of the people's rights.

I have never met a politician in Washington, or any American for that matter, who chose to be called "unpatriotic." Nor have I met anyone who did not believe he wholeheartedly supported our troops wherever they may be.

What I have heard all too frequently from various individuals is sharp accusations that because their political opponents disagree with them on the need for foreign military entanglements, they were "unpatriotic, un-American, evil doers deserving contempt."

The original American patriots were those individuals brave enough to resist with force the oppressive power of King George. I accept the definition of patriotism as that effort to resist oppressive state power. The true patriot is motivated by a sense of responsibility, and out of self interest -- for himself, his family, and the future of his country -- to resist government abuse of power. He rejects the notion that patriotism means obedience to the state.

Resistance need not be violent, but the civil disobedience that might be required involves confrontation with the state and invites possible imprisonment.

Peaceful non-violent revolutions against tyranny have

been every bit as successful as those involving military confrontation.   Mahatma Gandhi and Dr. Martin Luther King, Jr. achieved great political successes by practicing non-violence, yet they themselves suffered physically at the hands of the state.

But whether the resistance against government tyrants is non-violent or physically violent, the effort to over-throw state oppression qualifies as true patriotism.

True patriotism today has gotten a bad name—at least from the government and the press. Those who now challenge the unconstitutional methods of imposing an income tax on us, or force us to use a monetary sys-tem designed to serve the rich at the expense of the poor, are routinely condemned.   These American patriots are sadly looked down upon by many.   They are never praised as champions of liberty as Gandhi and Martin Luther King Jr. have been.

Liberals, who withhold their taxes as a protest against

war, are vilified as well—especially by conservative statists.

Unquestioned loyalty to the state is especially demanded in times of war. Lack of support for a war policy is said to be unpatriotic. Arguments against a particular policy that endorses a war once started, are always said to be endangering the troops in the field. This, they blatantly claim, is unpatriotic and all dissent must stop. Yet it is dissent from government policies that defines the true patriot and champion of liberty.

It is conveniently ignored that the only authentic way to best support the troops is to keep them out of dangerous, undeclared, no-win wars that are politically inspired. Sending troops off to war for reasons that are not truly related to national security -- and for that matter may even damage our security -- is hardly a way to "patriotically" support the troops.

Who are the true patriots: those who conform or those who protest against wars without purpose? How can it be said that blind support for war, no matter how misdirected the policy, is the duty of the patriot?

Randolph Bourne said that "war is the health of the state." With war, he argued, the state thrives. Those who believe in the powerful state see war as an opportunity. Those who mistrust the people and the market for solving problems have no trouble promoting a "war psychology" to justify the expansive role of the state.

This includes the role the federal government plays in our personal lives as well as in all our economic transactions. And certainly the neo-conservative belief that we have a moral obligation to spread American values worldwide, through force, justifies the conditions of war in order to rally support at home for the heavy hand of government. It is through this policy, it should surprise no one, that our liberties are undermined, the economy becomes overextended, and our involvement worldwide becomes prohibitive.

Out of fear of being labeled unpatriotic, most citizens become compliant and accept the argument that some loss of liberty is required to fight the war in order to remain safe. This is a bad trade-off in my estimation, especially when done in the name of patriotism.

Loyalty to the state and to autocratic leaders is substituted for true patriotism—that is, a willingness to challenge the state and defend the country, the people, and the culture. The more difficult the times, the stronger the admonition becomes that the leaders be not criticized.

Because the crisis atmosphere of war supports the growth of the state, any problem invites an answer by declaring "war" -- even on social and economic issues. This elicits patriotism in support of various government solutions while enhancing the power of the state. Faith in government coercion and a lack of understanding of how free societies operate, encourages big government liberals and big government conservatives to manufacture a war psychology to demand political loyalty for domestic policy just as is required in foreign affairs. The long term cost in dollars spent and liberties lost is neglected as immediate needs are emphasized.

It is for this reason that we have multiple perpetual wars going on simultaneously. Thus the war on drugs, against gun ownership, poverty, illiteracy, and terrorism, as well as our foreign military entanglements, are endless.

All this effort promotes the growth of statism at the expense of liberty. A government designed for a free society should do the opposite: prevent the growth of statism and preserve liberty. Once a war of any sort is declared, the message is sent out not to object or you will be declared unpatriotic. Yet, we must not forget that the true patriot is the one who protests in spite of the consequences, condemnation or ostracism, or even imprisonment that may result.

Non-violent protesters of the tax code are frequently imprisoned—whether they are protesting the code's unconstitutionality or the war that the tax revenues are funding.

Resisters to the military draft, or even to selective service registration, are threatened and imprisoned for challenging this threat to liberty.

Statism depends on the idea that the government owns us and citizens must obey. Confiscating the fruits of our labor through the income tax is crucial to the health of the state. The draft, or even the mere existence of the selective service, emphasizes that we will march off to war at the state's pleasure. A free society rejects all notions of involuntary servitude whether by draft or the confiscation of the fruits of our labor through the personal income tax.

A more sophisticated and less well known technique for enhancing the state is the manipulation and transfer of wealth through the fiat monetary system operated by the secretive Federal Reserve. Protesters against this unconstitutional system of paper money are considered unpatriotic criminals and at times are imprisoned for their beliefs. The fact that, according to the Constitution, only gold and silver are legal tender and paper money is outlawed, matters little. The principle of patriotism is turned on its head.

Whether it's with regard to the defense of welfare spending at home, confiscatory income tax, an immoral monetary system, or support for a war fought under false pretense without a legal declaration, the defenders of liberty and the Constitution are portrayed as unpatriotic while those who support these programs are seen as the patriots. If there's a "war" going on, supporting the state's efforts to win the war is expected at all costs. No dissent!

The real problem is that those who love the state too often advocate policies that lead to military action. At home they are quite willing to produce a crisis atmosphere and claim a war is needed to solve the problem. Under these conditions the people are more willing to bear the burden of paying for the war, and to carelessly sacrifice liberties which they are told is necessary.

The last six years have been quite beneficial to the "health of the state," which comes at the expense of personal liberty. Every enhanced unconstitutional power of the state can only be achieved at the expense of individual liberty.

Even though every war in which we have been engaged civil liberties have suffered, some have been restored after the war ended, but never completely. This has resulted in a steady erosion of our liberties over the past 200 years. Our government was originally designed to protect our liberties, but it has now instead become the usurper of those liberties.

We currently live in the most difficult of times for guarding against an expanding central government with a steady erosion of our freedoms.

We are continually being reminded that "9/11 has changed everything." Unfortunately, the policy that needed most to be changed—that is our policy of foreign interventionism—has only been expanded. There is no pretense any longer that a policy of humility in foreign affairs, without being the world's policeman and engaging in nation building, is worthy of consideration. We now live in a post 9/11 America where our government is going to make us safe no matter what it takes. We're expected to grin and bear it and adjust to every loss of our liberties in the name of patriotism and security.

Though the majority of Americans initially welcomed

this declared effort to make us safe, and were willing
to sacrifice for the cause, more and more Americans
are now becoming concerned about civil liberties
being needlessly and dangerously sacrificed. The
problem is that the Iraq war continues to drag on and
a real danger of its spreading exists. There's no evidence that a truce will soon be signed in Iraq , or in the
war on terror or drugs. Victory is not even definable.
If Congress is incapable of declaring an official war,
it's impossible to know when it will end. We have
been fully forewarned that the world conflict in which
we're now engaged will last a long, long time.

The war mentality, and the pervasive fear of an
unidentified enemy, allows for a steady erosion of our
liberties, and with this our respect for self reliance and
confidence is lost. Just think of the self sacrifice and
the humiliation we go through at the airport screening
process on a routine basis. Though there's no scientific evidence of any likelihood of liquids and gels
being mixed on an airplane to make a bomb, billions
of dollars are wasted throwing away toothpaste and

hairspray and searching old women in wheelchairs.

Our enemies say boo, and we jump, we panic, and then we punish ourselves. We're worse than a child being afraid of the dark. But in a way, the fear of indefinable terrorism is based on our inability to admit the truth about why there is a desire by a small number of angry radical Islamics to kill Americans. It's certainly not all because they are jealous of our wealth and freedoms.

We fail to realize that the extremists, willing to sacrifice their own lives to kill their enemies, do so out of a sense of weakness and desperation over real and perceived attacks on their way of life, their religion, their country and their natural resources. Without the conventional diplomatic or military means to retaliate against these attacks, and an unwillingness of their own government to address the issue, they resort to the desperation tactic of suicide terrorism. Their anger toward their own governments, which they believe are co-conspirators with the American government, is equal to or greater than that directed toward us. These errors in judgment in understanding the motive of the enemy and the constant fear that is generated have brought us to this crisis where our civil liberties and privacy are being steadily eroded in the name of preserving national security. We may be the economic and military giant of the world, but the effort to stop this war on our liberties here at home in the name of patriotism, is being lost.

The erosion of our personal liberties started long before 9/11, but 9/11 accelerated the process. There are many things that motivate those who pursue this course—both well-intentioned and malevolent. But it would not happen if the people remained vigilant, understood the importance of individual rights, and were unpersuaded that a need for security justifies the sacrifice of liberty—even if it's just now and then.

The true patriot challenges the state when the state

embarks on enhancing its power at the expense of the individual. Without a better understanding and a greater determination to reign in the state, the rights of Americans that resulted from the revolutionary break from the British and the writing of the Constitution, will disappear.

The record since September 11, 2001, is dismal. Respect for liberty has rapidly deteriorated.

Many of the new laws passed after 9/11 had in fact been proposed long before that attack. The political atmosphere after that attack simply made it more possible to pass such legislation. The fear generated by 9/11 became an opportunity for those seeking to promote the power of the state domestically, just as it served to falsely justify the long planned-for invasion of Iraq .

The war mentality was generated by the Iraq war in combination with the constant drum beat of fear at home. Al Qaeda and Osama bin Laden, who is now likely residing in Pakistan , our supposed ally, are ignored, as our troops fight and die in Iraq and are made easier targets for the terrorists in their backyard. While our leaders constantly use the mess we created to further justify the erosion of our constitutional rights here at home, we forget about our own borders and support the inexorable move toward global government—hardly a good plan for America.

The accelerated attacks on liberty started quickly after 9/11. Within weeks the Patriot Act was overwhelmingly passed by Congress. Though the final version was unavailable up to a few hours before the vote—no Member had sufficient time to read or understand it— political fear of "not doing something," even something harmful, drove Members of Congress to not question the contents and just vote for it. A little less freedom for a little more perceived safety was considered a fair trade off—and the majority of Americans applauded.

The Patriot Act, though, severely eroded the system of checks and balances by giving the state the power to spy on law abiding citizens without judicial supervision. The several provisions that undermine the liberties of all Americans include: sneak and peak searches; a broadened and more vague definition of domestic terrorism; allowing the FBI access to libraries and bookstore records without search warrants or probable cause; easier FBI initiation of wiretaps and searches, as well as roving wiretaps; easier access to information on American citizens' use of the Internet; and easier access to e-mail and financial records of all American citizens.

The attack on privacy has not relented over the past six years. The Military Commissions Act is a particularly egregious piece of legislation and, if not repealed, will change America for the worse as the powers unconstitutionally granted to the Executive Branch are used and abused.

This act grants excessive authority to use secretive military commissions outside of places where active hostilities are going on. The Military Commissions Act permits torture, arbitrary detention of American citizens as unlawful enemy combatants at the full discretion of the President and without the right of Habeas Corpus, and warrantless searches by the NSA (National Security Agency). It also gives to the President the power to imprison individuals based on secret testimony.

Since 9/11, Presidential signing statements designating portions of legislation that the President does not intend to follow, though not legal under the Constitution, have enormously multiplied. Unconstitutional Executive Orders are numerous and mischievous and need to be curtailed.

Extraordinary rendition to secret prisons around the world has been widely engaged in, though obviously extra-legal.

A growing concern in the post 9/11 environment is the federal government's lists of potential terrorists based on secret evidence. Mistakes are made and sometimes it is virtually impossible to get one's name removed, even though the accused is totally innocent of any wrongdoing.

A national ID card is now in the process of being implemented. It's called the Real ID card and it's tied to our Social Security numbers and our state driver's license. If Real ID is not stopped it will become a national driver's license/ID for all America .

Some of the least noticed and least discussed changes in the law were the changes made to the Insurrection Act of 1807 and to Posse Comitatus by the Defense Authorization Act of 2007.

These changes pose a threat to the survival of our republic by giving the President the power to declare martial law for as little reason as to restore "public order." The 1807 Act severely restricted the President in his use of the military within the United States borders, and the Posse Comitatus Act of 1878 strengthened these restrictions with strict oversight by Congress. The new law allows the President to circumvent the restrictions of both laws. The Insurrection Act has now become the "Enforcement of the Laws to Restore Public Order Act". This is hardly a title that suggests that the authors cared about or understood the nature of a constitutional republic.

Now, martial law can be declared not just for "insurrection" but also for "natural disasters, public health reasons, terrorist attacks or incidents" or for the vague reason called "other conditions." The President can call up the National Guard without Congressional approval or the governors' approval and even send these state guard troops into other states. The American republic is in remnant status. The stage is set for

our country eventually devolving into a military dictatorship and few seem to care.

These precedent setting changes in the law are
extremely dangerous and will change American
jurisprudence forever if not reversed. The beneficial
results of our revolt against the king's abuses are about
to be eliminated and few Members of Congress and
few Americans are aware of the seriousness of the situation. Complacency and fear drive our legislation
without any serious objection by our elected leaders.

Sadly, those few who do object to this self evident
trend away from personal liberty and empire building
overseas are portrayed as unpatriotic and uncaring.

Though welfare and socialism always fails, opponents
of them are labeled uncaring. Though opposition to
totally unnecessary war should be the only moral position, the rhetoric is twisted to claim that patriots who
oppose the war are not "supporting the troops". The

cliché "support the troops" is incessantly used as a substitute for the unacceptable notion of "supporting the policy" no matter how flawed it may be. Unsound policy can never help the troops. Keeping the troops out of harm's way and out of wars unrelated to our national security is the only real way of protecting the troops. With this understanding, just who can claim the title of "patriot"?

Before the war in the Middle East spreads and becomes a world conflict, for which we'll be held responsible, or the liberties of all Americans become so suppressed we can no longer resist, much has to be done. Time is short but our course of action should be clear. Resistance to illegal and unconstitutional usurpation of our rights is required. Each of us must choose which course of action we should take—education, conventional political action, or even peaceful civil disobedience, to bring about the necessary changes.

But let it not be said that we did nothing.

Let not those who love the power of the welfare/warfare state label the dissenters of authoritarianism as unpatriotic or uncaring. Patriotism is more closely linked to dissent than it is to conformity and a blind desire for safety and security. Understanding the magnificent rewards of a free society makes us unbashful in its promotion, fully realizing that maximum wealth is created and the greatest chance for peace comes from a society respectful of individual liberty.

Cong. Rec. 22 May, 2007: H5609-H5612

A Breath of Air

Ron Paul's candidacy represents the movement with the greatest chance of saving America from collapse. Barak Obama says he is the candidate of change; Mitt Romney says he is the candidate of change; in a sense, both of them are correct, however Ron Paul is taking the fire out of their campaigns because he represents real fundamental change to a degree which has not been seen since the New Deal.

Bureaucracies never add freedoms, they always slowly eat away at them. The federal government has failed on so many levels, it is filled with functionaries pushing paper and absorbing the products of our economy.

In the long run, the government will probably resume its path towards totalitarianism, but Ron Paul can be a refresher. A Ron Paul presidency will put off our national collapse for a few years and provide some excellent entertainment. We can all watch as Ron Paul vetoes everything that comes across his desk, and shuts down the federal government entirely. Hopefully he won't go so far as to auction off the contents of the Smithsonian and Yellowstone National Park, and hopefully he won't shut down some of the more benign government agencies, such as the Peace Corps and the Post Office.

Ron Paul has the potential to secure civil liberties for all Americans, actually reduce government spending for the first time in nearly a century, and restore our republic as a government of laws, not a government of men. As the Internet becomes a central part of the lives of more and more Americans, the real world will continue to be reshaped in its image to greater and greater extents. The power of Ron Paul's candidacy has brought this to the fore. Will we see a continued decline towards totalitarianism, or will we see the rebirth of personal responsibility? The power of the Internet will be tested and the answer will be visible for all to see. Ron Paul will keep speaking of Freedom.

Made in the USA